Carl Philipp Emanuel Bach
Johann Friedrich Agricola
Lorenz Christoph Mizler
Walter Emery

Nekrolog
or
Obituary Notice
of
Johann Sebastian Bach.

Published Travis & Emery 2009.
Travis & Emery Music Bookshop
17 Cecil Court, London, WC2N 4EZ, United Kingdom.
Tel. (+44) 20 7240 2129
neworders@travis-and-emery.com

ISBN Hardback: 978-1-906857-79-0 Paperback: 978-1-906857-80-6

THE NEKROLOG

THE NEKROLOG OR
OBITUARY NOTICE OF
JOHANN SEBASTIAN BACH
TRANSLATED INTO ENGLISH
WITH AN INTRODUCTION
NOTES AND TWO
APPENDICES
BY WALTER EMERY

MCMXLII

CONTENTS

TO BETTY: 29 MARCH 1942

IT MAY ONE DAY be my misfortune to have to
deal biographically with Bach, as an introduction
to the study of his organ works that I hope in
time to find material for. Even if I never rise so
high, I must still make myself acquainted with
the facts of his life; not that I expect to find
therein any confirmation of the vulgar notion that
a composer writes a love-song because he has just
found a new mistress (for that matter, the old boy

does not seem to have indulged in such luxuries);
but an editor never knows when some odd bit of
apparently disconnected information will fall
into place and settle a problem.

For my purpose I must not only read up the
material that passes for Bach biography in the
works of the standard authors; I must know how
much of this material is solid fact (i.e., directly
drawn from such documents as the registers of
churches, courts, and town councils), how much
is reasonably likely to be true (e.g., statements of
authors up to the time of Forkel, most, if not all,

of whom were acquainted with Bach either themselves or at only one remove), and how much is
mere guesswork, provided by later biographers
in order to connect or explain the facts at their
disposal. (I am not attempting to disparage
the work of the standard authors. A vast amount
of such guesswork is essential, and much of
what has been done must come near the truth.)
An obvious step in this necessary inquiry is to
read all the early writings on Bach (which, thank
the Lord, are not so very numerous), and this
I have begun to do.

THE NEKROLOG

The first notice of Bach in a reference book is the article in Walther's LEXICON of 1732, of which I give a translation in Appendix I.

Then there is the bare outline of Bach's life up to c. 1736 given in the Genealogy (Appendix II).

About this time there appeared some casual references to Bach and his works, and Scheibe made his attack on Bach — the beginning of a series of tedious controversial articles which nevertheless contains some important matter. These writings are not at present available to me

(I was fool enough not to buy the Scheibe when I
had the chance), and to go into them properly
will involve work in the British Museum. They
are therefore not dealt with here.

Then in 1754, four years after Bach's death,
appeared his belated obituary notice, commonly
known as the NEKROLOG. The translation of
this forms the bulk of the present book.

On each of these texts I have commented
either in the Introduction or the Notes. The latter
are a very mixed bag. Some are essential cor-
rections. Some contain additional matter that

I thought might interest you. One or two merely record guesses of my own, which need to be backed up by more evidence before they can be published, but which I don't want to forget. At one time I intended to make the notes very much more comprehensive, and to include among them general discussions of the music and the way in which Bach's style changed as he grew older, came under new influences, and found at his disposal new instrumental and vocal media; but I came to the conclusion that without reference books this would be impossible;

DEDICATORY NOTE vii

and further, as at present I have little to add
to the writings of the standard authors, I should
for the most part have been simply re-hashing
well-known material. The result would have
justified neither the labour involved nor the risk
of damaging my not valueless books by keeping
them in the conditions I am at present living
in.

Most of the translation was done last winter.
Mrs Cocker at Novellos helped me with some of
the more contorted sentences; but there were some
that puzzled her and others that I forgot to ask

her about. However, the translation (though by
no means literal) is as accurate as I can make
it; and indeed I think that in the prose the
sense of it is right enough: what I have missed
here and there is the exact meaning of such
phrases as 'auf das Verdienst seines Er-
lösers ... verschied' – obviously a pious
euphemism which it would have been pleasant
to translate instead of using the bald 'died'.
As for the LIBRETTO at the end, I have had
no help with it at all (except that you have
given me the dictionary meanings of certain

words), and have had to guess a good deal. Fortunately the thing is of no importance, whether as biography or literature.

The Introduction and Notes are of a rather formal cast because I might one day publish the work more or less as it stands, but with the addition of the other early writings that I cannot deal with at present; and I thought I might as well get the material into shape and be done with it.

Now read the Postscript (p. 227). I am sorry

that I could not finish the job in time for Christmas (my original intention); but anyway,
here it is. It has done me good, and I hope
you will find this account of the Trials of
an Organist not unamusing in parts.

INTRODUCTION

THE SO-CALLED NEKROLOG appeared in the last number issued of Lorenz Christoph Mizler's NEU ERÖFFNETER MUSIKAL - ISCHER BIBLIOTHEK (Bd. iv, Teil i, Leipzig 1754); this was the official organ of the Society of Musical Sciences founded by Mizler. The authors' names are not given; but in a letter to Forkel dated 13 Jan. 1775 Emanuel Bach says, 'The account of my

late father's life in Mizler, dearest friend, was
put together by the late Agricola and myself
in Berlin; Mizler added to it only the portion
that begins at the words "He joined the Society"
and continues to the end. It is not worth much.
The deceased, like myself and all true musicians, was no lover of dry mathematical
matters."[x]

Philipp Emanuel Bach, Sebastian's second
son, lived at home until 1734. Johann
Friedrich Agricola was a pupil of Bach's from

[x] Bach-Urkunden, N.B.G. xvii, 3; 1917.

1738 to 1741. Owing to its authorship, therefore, and despite its occasional errors, the Nekrolog is a historical document of some importance. It was the first attempt at a full-length biography of Bach and a critical appreciation of his work as composer and performer (the notice in Walther's LEXICON of 1732 being necessarily incomplete); and directly or indirectly it has been used by all subsequent biographers.

The earlier parts of the MUSIKALISCHER BIBLIOTHEK are not uncommon books;

but Band iv Teil i, a small book and easily
lost, has become something of a rarity. (I have
been unable to trace a copy in England.)
Despite this fact and the importance of the
Nekrolog, the full text of the latter was never
reprinted until 1920[x], when B.F. Richter edited
it for the Bach-Jahrbuch. The present is the
first English translation: a free version based
on Richter's text, but including the Canon,
which he omitted. I regret that my ability

[x] The LIBRETTO appeared in Bitter's biography,
1st edition, 1865.

as a versifier does not enable me to do justice to
Dr Georg Wenzky's LIBRETTO.

As Appendices I give translations of the
article on Bach in Johann Gottfried Walther's
MUSIKALISCHES LEXICON (1732), and the
entry concerning him in the Genealogy (the
wording probably Sebastian's own, and the date
of the entry c. 1736).

Square brackets indicate editorial additions
and alterations. The small superimposed figures
refer to the Notes at the end of the book. I have
altered old-fashioned spellings of place- and

personal names to agree with those now in common use, and have taken some 'typographical' liberties.

It looks as if the biographical portions of the Nekrolog (exasperatingly meagre, considering the unrivalled advantages enjoyed by its authors) were based on the Genealogy; Emanuel had a copy of this, and both texts give an incorrect date for Bach's appointment to Arnstadt. Musically, Emanuel and Agricola were more concerned with the excellence of Bach's organ- and clavier-playing than with that of his compositions. To-day our attitude is very much the reverse. Fortunately the purely musical critics, unlike the pure biographers and the miserable textual critics, have plenty of material to work on — the forty-odd fat volumes of the B.G.; and there is no need to expatiate here on the well-known characteristics of Bach's works, or on their musical value.

In compiling the Notes I was chiefly concerned to correct and comment on the Nekrolog's errors; but I have provided some

extra information, so that the book as a whole
may serve as a short biography, of peculiar
interest owing to its origin, from which the
interested reader may pass on to the more
elaborate studies for which we have to
thank the labours of more modern authors.

THE TEXT OF THE NEKROLOG

[MIZLER records the deaths of Georg
Heinrich Bümler and Gottfried Heinrich
Stölzel, and continues:]

THE THIRD AND LAST IS THE HIGH-
BORN HERR JOHANN SEBASTIAN BACH,
WORLD-RENOWNED AS AN ORGANIST,
COURT COMPOSER TO THE KING OF
POLAND AND ELECTOR OF SAXONY,
AND DIRECTOR OF MUSIC IN LEIPZIG.

JOHANN SEBASTIAN BACH belonged to a
family whose every member seems to have had,
as a natural gift, a fondness for music and

ability in its practice. At least it is certain
that, from the founder of the family (Veit
Bach) to his descendants of the seventh
and present generation, all the Bachs
have been devoted to music; and further,
with one or two possible exceptions, they
have all made it their profession.[1] This
Veit was exiled from Hungary in the sixteenth
century, for religious reasons; he later settled
in Thuringia, in which province a number
of his descendants also have made their
homes.[2]

Among the many members of the Bach
family that have distinguished themselves
in the practice of music, or the construction
of new musical instruments, the following
(besides our Johann Sebastian) are particularly
remarkable as having been composers:

1 Heinrich Bach [b.1615], organist at
Arnstadt, who died in 1692

2 and 3   his two sons: Johann Christoph
[b. 1642], Court and Town Organist at
Eisenach, who died in 1703: and Johann
Michael [1648-94], organist and parish

clerk in the Gehren district, who was Johann
Sebastian's first father-in-law

4 Johann Ludwig Bach [1677 - 1741],
Ducal Capellmeister at Meiningen

5 Johann Bernhard Bach [b. 1676],
chamber-musician and organist at Eisenach, who passed away in 1749.

Ample evidence of all these men's ability
as composers, both in vocal and instrumental
forms, is provided by their extant works. The
above-mentioned Johann Christoph, especially, had a gift for the invention of

beautiful themes, as well as for setting words
expressively. He composed (so far, that is, as
the taste of his day would permit) both in
the galant or singing style and in extraordinarily full polyphony. The first statement
is borne out by a motet of his, composed
more than seventy years ago; at which early
date, apart from other striking touches, he
was bold enough to use the chord of the
augmented sixth. As for the second statement, he composed a Church Cantata in
twenty-two obbligato parts, whose harmony is

nevertheless flawlessly pure throughout; and it is equally noteworthy that on the organ and clavier he never played in less than five real parts.[3]

Johann Bernhard composed a number of fine overtures in the Telemann style.

It would seem strange that men so worthy should have remained so little known outside their own province, did we not remember that these honest Thuringians were so content with their fatherland and their circumstances that never once would they venture upon following

their fortune far away. The applause of the
noblemen in whose domains they were born,
and that of a host of their simple - hearted
fellow - countrymen, was theirs already; and
this they greatly preferred to the encomiums,
to be won (if at all) only with difficulty and
expense, of strangers fewer in. number and
most probably envious. It is, meanwhile,
our duty to refresh and keep green the memory
of worthy men ; and this will amply justify
us before those who may, perhaps, think this
little digression upon the musical history of

the Bach family too long and detailed. We
return to our Johann Sebastian.[4]

HE WAS BORN AT EISENACH on 21 Mar.
1685[5]. His parents were Johann Ambrosius
Bach, Court and Town Musician there, and
Elisabeth (née Lämmerhirt), whose father
was an alderman at Erfurt[6]. Sebastian's
father had a twin brother named Johann
Christoph[7], who was a Court and Town Musician at Arnstadt. These two brothers were
so alike in everything — even to the state of

their health and their musical ability — that
when they were together they could be told apart
only by their clothes.

Johann Sebastian found himself orphaned
before he was ten years old. He moved to Ohrdruf, and was taken in by his eldest brother
Johann Christoph[8], who was organist there;
under the latter's guidance he laid the found-
ations of his clavier technique. Our little
Johann Sebastian was, even at that tender
age, extraordinarily eager to extend his
knowledge of music. In a very short time he

mastered all the pieces that his brother was
willing to give him for his instruction; but
his brother had also a book full of clavier
works by the then celebrated masters Fro-
berger, Kerl, and Pachelbel; and this, despite all his entreaties, was forbidden to him.
Who knows why? In his eagerness to make
further progress he thought of the following
innocent trick: The book was kept in a
cupboard, which had only a latticed door.
With his small hands he was able to reach
through the lattice, and, as the book was bound

in paper only, to roll it up and withdraw it.
This he did at night, when all were in bed;
and as he was never able to strike a light,
he copied the book by moonlight. After six
months this musical prize was safely in his
hands, and with the greatest eagerness he
attempted to make use of it in secret; but,
to his intense distress, his brother found
him out and unmercifully deprived him of
his copy, made with such great labour. To
appreciate our little Johann Sebastian's
grief over this loss, we have only to think of

a miser that has lost a ship on the way to
Peru with a hundred thousand thalers. He
did not regain the book until after his -
brother's death? And is it not possible that
this very anxiety to make progress in music,
and the labour expended upon the book in
question, were incidentally responsible for
his death? as we shall see later.
After his brother died
[In the year 1700] Johann Sebastian betook
himself to St. Michael's Gymnasium at
Lüneburg, in company with a schoolfellow
of his named Erdmann; who died, not

very many years ago, at Danzig, as a Baron
and Resident of the Tsar of Russia's.[10]

Our Bach was well received at Lüneburg,
on account of his unusually fine soprano
voice. Some time afterwards, in the choir one
day, he found himself singing, besides the
soprano notes that he was supposed to produce,
those an octave lower at the same time; and
this unconsciously,. and indeed against his
will. His voice behaved in this quite new way
for eight days, during which time he could
neither speak nor sing but in octaves. After

that he lost the soprano notes, and therewith
his fine voice.

From Lüneburg he sometimes made his way
to Hamburg, to hear the then celebrated
organist of St. Catherine's Church, Johann
Adam Reinken. Here also he had the opportunity of becoming thoroughly familiar with
the French style; which at that time and in
that neighbourhood was quite new, by
frequent listening to a band, then famous,
maintained by the Duke of Celle and consisting for the most part of Frenchmen."

In 1703 he came to Weimar[12], and became a Court Musician there. Later in the same year he was appointed organist of the New Church at Arnstadt[13]. Here he displayed the real first-fruits of his diligent study of the arts of organ-playing and composition; which latter he had learnt, for the most part, only from examining the works of composers then famous and regarded as profound, and putting into practice the results of his study. In his organ compositions he took as models the works of Bruhns, Reinken, Buxtehude,

and certain good French organists[4]. He was
particularly desirous of hearing good
organists as much as he possibly could;
and here at Arnstadt this desire moved him
to set out for Lübeck[15] — what is more, on
foot — to hear Dietrich Buxtehude, the
famous organist of St. Mary's Church in
that city. He stayed at Lübeck, not without
profit, for nearly three months; not until then
did he turn back to Arnstadt.

In 1707 he was appointed organist of the
church of St. Blasius, Mühlhausen[16]. This

town, however, was not to have the satisfaction
of keeping him long; for in the following year
a visit to Weimar brought with it an opportunity of playing before the Duke; the result
was that he was offered a position as chamber
[musician] and Court Organist : an offer
that he immediately accepted[7]. His gracious
master's delight in his playing encouraged
him to exert himself to the utmost to master
the art of managing the organ; and it was
here that he composed most of his organ works[8].
In 1714 he was made Concertmeister at the

same Court ; but as such his duties at that time consisted chiefly in composing and performing Church Cantatas[19]. At Weimar he trained not a few competent organists; among whom Johann Caspar Vogler, his second successor at Weimar itself, is most deserving of mention.

After the death of Zachau, Director of Music and Organist at the Market Church in Halle, our Bach received an invitation to that post. He did in fact visit Halle, and performed a test-piece there; but he found

good reasons for refusing the post, which was
afterwards obtained by Kirchhof.[20]

   In 1717 our Bach, already so famous, had
a further opportunity of adding to his renown.
Marchand, celebrated in France as a clavier-
player and organist, had come to Dresden
and played before the King to the latter's particular satisfaction; and had been so fortunate
as to be offered a position at Court with a
generous salary. Volumier, who was then
Concertmeister at Dresden, was not unacquaint-
ed with Bach's merits; and wrote to him at

Weimar, inviting him to come to Dresden without delay and challenge the arrogant Marchand to a musical contest for the preëminence. Bach readily accepted this invitation, and set out for Dresden. Volumier received him with open arms, and arranged for him to hear his opponent beforehand, in secret. After this Bach invited Marchand to the contest in a courteous private letter, wherein he professed his readiness to perform extempore any musical task that Marchand should set him, if Marchand would do the same in return.

Great audacity, to be sure! Marchand readily
accepted the challenge. Time and place were
settled, not without the King's knowledge; and
at the appointed time Bach was to be found
on the field of battle, in the house of a certain
eminent minister, where there was gathered
a great company of persons, of high rank and
of both sexes. They waited long for Marchand.
Finally, the owner of the house sent to Marchand's lodgings to remind him, in case he
should have forgotten, that now was the time
to show himself a man. But, to their great

surprise, they found that early in the morning
of that same day Monsieur Marchand had
left Dresden by special post. Bach, thus left
sole master of the field, had in consequence
opportunity enough of demonstrating the
strength with which he was armed against
his opponent; and this he did, to the wonder
of all those present. As a reward, the King
set aside for him a present of 500 thalers;
but of this he was deprived through the dis-
honesty of a certain official, who thought he
could make a better use of this present; and

had to return home with the honour he had
acquired as the sole return for his labours.
A strange fatality! A Frenchman voluntarily
forsakes the substantial salary (of more than
a thousand thalers) that was offered him;
and the German whom, as is obvious from his
flight, he regarded as his superior, cannot
obtain so much as part of the single present
destined for him by the King's bounty! For
the rest, our Bach freely admitted that Marchand
was a neat and fine executant; but whether
Marchand's *Musettes for Christmas Night*,

whose composition and performance had won him the greatest fame in Paris, would before connoisseurs have been able to hold their own against the manifold variety of Bach's fugues, let them decide who heard them both in their strength.[21]

After our Bach's return to Weimar, and still in the same year, he was appointed Capellmeister to Leopold, at that time Prince of Anhalt-Cöthen, and a great connoisseur and lover of music.[22] He entered upon his duties immediately, and discharged them,

to the very great satisfaction of his gracious
prince, for nearly six years. During this time,
in about the year 1722[23], he visited Hamburg;
and there played, to the general wonderment,
for more than two hours upon the fine organ
of St. Catharine's Church, before the magistracy and many other notables of the town.
The old organist of this church, Johann Adam
Reinken (who at that time was nearly a
hundred years of age), listened to him with
particular satisfaction, and paid him the
following compliment, "I thought this art

was dead; but I see that it yet lives in you'— referring especially to the chorale 'An Wasserflüssen Babylon', upon which our Bach had, at the request of those present, extemporized at great length (for nearly half an hour) and in various styles, just as in former days the best of the Hamburg organists had been accustomed to do at Sunday Vespers. Such appreciation was the less to be expected of Reinken because, many years before, he had worked out this very chorale in the very same style; which,

as also the fact that he had always been somewhat envious, was not unknown to our Bach.
With this, Reinken invited Bach to his house,
and treated him with great courtesy.

In 1723 the town of Leipzig chose our Bach
as their Director of Music and Cantor of St
Thomas' School.[24] He accepted this invitation,
although it was with reluctance that he left his
gracious Prince. It seems as if Providence
wished to remove him from Cöthen before the death
of the Prince which, contrary to all expectation,
took place shortly afterwards[25]; in this way he

was at least no longer compelled to be actually
present at this sad event. He had, however,
the melancholy satisfaction of composing,
while at Leipzig, the funeral music for his
so dearly beloved Prince, and of performing
it in person at Cöthen.

Not long after this, he was appointed
Capellmeister to the Duke of Weissenfels; and
in 1736 he was made Court Composer to the
King of Poland and Elector of Saxony, having
some time previously played the organ in public
at Dresden, before the Court and the musical

connoisseurs of the town, with great applause.[26]

In 1747 he visited Berlin, and it was on this occasion that he received the honour of playing before His Majesty the King of Prussia at Potsdam. His Majesty himself played over to him a theme for a fugue, which, to His Majesty's very great satisfaction, he immediately worked out on the pianoforte. Thereupon His Majesty expressed a desire to hear a fugue with six obbligato parts; and this command also he immediately carried out upon a theme of his own choice, to the wonder of the King

and the musicians present. After his return
to Leipzig he wrote out two Ricercars (so
called), one in three parts, the other in six,
together with certain other smaller works, all
upon the theme given him by His Majesty;
had them engraved upon copper, and dedicated them to the King.[27]

His sight, naturally somewhat weak, had
been still further impaired by his unheard-
of zeal for study, at which, especially in
his youth, he would sit up all night; and
the result was that in his last years his eyes

became diseased. Partly from a desire to con-
tinue to serve God and his neighbour — his
mental and bodily powers being otherwise still
very brisk — and partly on the advice of certain
friends, who put much faith in an eye-doctor
who had just arrived in Leipzig, he wished to
obtain relief by an operation. This, however,
had to be repeated; and even so it turned out
very badly. Not only did he not regain his
sight; but also his health, otherwise extremely
sound, was completely broken down by the operation and the injurious medicines and treatment

associated with it; so that for fully six months
thereafter he was nearly always unwell. Ten
days before his death his eyes seemed suddenly
to improve, so that one morning he could
again see perfectly well, and bear the light.
But a few hours later he was struck down with
apoplexy; and upon this followed a high
fever, of which, despite the utmost care of
two of the most skilful doctors in Leipzig, he
died quietly and peacefully at a quarter to
nine in the evening of 28 July 1750, in his
sixty-sixth year.[28]

OF THE WORKS for which we have to thank this great composer, the following have been made available to the public by their being engraved:

1 Clavierübung [Clavier Exercises], First Part: consisting of six Suites

2 Clavierübung, Second Part: consisting of a Concerto and an Overture for a two-manual clavicembalo

3 Clavierübung, Third Part: consisting

of a number of preludes on certain chorales,
for organ

4 An Aria with Thirty Variations, for
[a clavicembalo with] two manuals

5 Six three-part Preludes, for [vor] the
same number of chorales, for organ

6 Certain Canonic Variations on the
chorale VOM HIMMEL HOCH DA KOMM ICH
HER

7 Two Fugues [Ricercars], a Trio, and a
number of Canons, on the above-mentioned
theme set by His Majesty the King of Prussia,

under the title of MUSICAL OFFERING

   8 THE ART OF FUGUE. This, the composer's last work, contains Counterpoints [i.e. Fugues] and Canons of all kinds upon a single main theme. His last illness prevented him from finishing what was to have been, according to plan, the penultimate fugue, and from composing the final one, which was to have had four subjects, and afterwards to have been inverted note for note in all four parts. This work was not published until after the late composer's death.[29]

The following is an approximate list of the late Bach's unpublished works:

1   Five annual cycles of Church Cantatas, for all Sundays and Feast-days

2   A number of Oratorios and Masses: a Magnificat: some settings of the Sanctus: Dramas, Serenades: music for birthdays, anniversaries, and funerals: music for weddings, and one or two comic Cantatas

3   Five Passions, of which one is for double choir

4   Some Motets for double choir

5 A large number of free Preludes, Fugues, and similar pieces, for the organ with obbligato pedal

6 Six Trios [Sonatas] for the organ with obbligato pedal

7 A number of Preludes for [vor] Chorales, for the organ

8 A book full of short Preludes for [vor] the majority of church hymns, for the organ

9 Two sets of Twenty-four Preludes and Fugues in all keys, for the clavier

10 Six Toccatas for the clavier

11 Six Suites ['English'] for the same

12 Six more of the same, somewhat shorter
[the 'French' Suites]

13 Six Sonatas for Violin, without bass

14 Six of the same for Violoncello

15 Sundry concertos for one, two, three,
and four clavicembalos

16 Finally, many other instrumental pieces,
of all kinds, and for all instruments.[30]

OUR BACH married twice. His first wife was
Maria Barbara, youngest daughter of the

above-mentioned Johann Michael Bach, a

noteworthy composer[31]. By her he had seven

five sons and two daughters,

children, among whom were a pair of twins.

Three of them are still alive, namely: the eldest

(unmarried) daughter, Catharina Dorothea,

born in 1708: Wilhelm Friedemann, born in

1710, now Director of Music and Organist of

the Market Church, Halle: and Carl Philipp

Emanuel, born in 1714, Chamber-musician

to the King of Prussia[32]. With this his first

wife he enjoyed thirteen years of contented

married life; but at Cöthen, in the year 1720,

he was overtaken by sore affliction: on his return from a journey to Carlsbad with his Prince, he found her dead and buried, although at his departure he had left her hale and hearty. He heard nothing of her illness and death until he entered his house.

At Cöthen, in 1721, he took his second wife: Anna Magdalena, youngest daughter of Herr Johann Caspar Wilcken, Court Trumpeter to the Duke of Weissenfels.[33] Of the thirteen children (six sons and seven daughters) whom she bore him, the following six are still alive : 1, Gottfried Heinrich, born in 1724 : 2, Elisabeth Juliane Fridrike, born in 1726; who is married to Herr Altnikol, organist of St. Wenceslas, Naumburg, and an able composer : 3, Johann Christoph Friedrich, born in 1732, now Chamber-musician to the High Count of the Empire [Wilhelm von] Schaumburg-Lippe : 4, Johann Christian, born in 1735 : 5, Johanna Carolina, born in 1737 : 6, Regina Susanna, born in 1742. The widow also is still alive.[34]

This is a very brief account of the life of a

man who proved a quite exceptional honour
to music, his fatherland, and his family.

IF EVER A COMPOSER displayed the full
power of polyphony, and made artistic use
of the most hidden mysteries of harmony,
then certainly our Bach did; none other
has infused such imaginative and various
life into these otherwise dry-seeming artifices.
He had but to hear a theme to realize instantly
how it could be subjected to artistic treatment.
His melodies were certainly peculiar; but

always different, full of invention, and unlike
those of any other composer. His serious temper-
ament inclined him chiefly to laborious, serious,
and profound music; yet he could also con-
descend, when necessary, to a light and
jocular manner, especially in his playing.
Constant practice in the composition of poly-
phonic works had given him so quick an eye
that he could grasp, at a glance, all the
simultaneously-sounding parts in the largest
scores. His ear was so keen that even in the
most complex music he was able to detect

the slightest error; it was unfortunate that he
seldom had the good fortune to find for his
works performers such as might have spared
him the necessity of making comments of this
disagreeable kind. In conducting he was very
accurate, and in his tempi (which he generally
took very fast) extremely certain.

So long as nothing can be brought against
us but the bare possibility that still better
organists and clavier-players have existed,
we cannot be blamed for being bold enough to
assert, still, that our BACH WAS THE GREAT-

EST ORGANIST AND CLAVIER-PLAYER
that has ever lived. No doubt many a
famous man has done great things in polyphony on these instruments; but was he therefore just as skilful — and moreover, as skilful
with hands and feet together — as our Bach[?].
Those who have had the pleasure of hearing him
as well as other players, and who are not otherwise prejudiced, will consider this doubt not
unfounded. And those who examine Bach's
organ and clavier works — which, as is generally
known, he himself performed without simplifications

or omissions — will likewise find little to set
against the above assertion. How strange, how
novel, how expressive, how beautiful were his
flights of fancy in extemporizing! how perfectly he expressed them! His fingers were all
exercised alike : all were equally equipped to
yield the utmost purity in performance. He had
devised for himself a system of fingering so
convenient that for him it was not hard to perform
the most difficult passages with the most flowing
ease. Before him, the most famous clavier-
players in Germany and other countries had

made little use of the thumb; he made all the
better use of it. With his two feet he could play
on the pedals passages that many a not un-
skilful clavier-player would have found hard
enough with his five fingers. Not only did he
understand the management of the organ
to perfection: how most fitly to combine stops
with each other, and how to show off each
stop to the best effect, according to its character;
he had also a thorough knowledge of organ-
building. This latter he once made more than
usually evident, at the examination of a new

organ in the church near which his remains
now rest. The builder of this organ was a man
in the last years of his long life. The examination was perhaps one of the most rigorous
ever made; consequently, the fact that Bach
publicly expressed his complete satisfaction
with the work by no means lessened the repute
either of the organ-builder or — owing to certain circumstances — of Bach himself.[35]

No-one was better able than he to work out
and criticize specifications for new organs.
Despite all this knowledge of the organ, he

was (as he would often complain) never so fortunate
as to have a really large and fine organ for his
own constant use. We have thus been deprived
of many beautiful and unheard compositions
for the organ[36], which otherwise he would have
committed to paper and set forth just as he
had them in his head. And, to omit other
merits that were his[37], in tuning the clavicembalo
he tempered it so purely and correctly that all
keys sounded well and pleasantly. He knew
of no key that had to be avoided because of
incorrect tuning.

For his moral character they can speak who
enjoyed his conversation and friendship, and
are become witnesses to his integrity before God
and his neighbour.

[38] He joined the Society of Musical Sciences
in June 1747, at the suggestion of Court Councill
or Mizler, whose good friend he was, and to
whom, when still studying in Leipzig, he had
given instruction in clavier-playing and composition. To be sure, our late Bach would have
nothing to do with deep theoretical speculations
about music; but he was all the stronger in

practical matters. He supplied the Society with the chorale VOM HIMMEL HOCH DA KOMM' ICH HER, completely worked out; it was afterwards engraved on copper. He had also submitted to the Society the Canon engraved on Tab. iv f. 16 [see p. 63],[39] and would certainly have done much more had he not been prevented by lack of time; for he was a member of the Society for only three years.

The LIBRETTO in his honour as a member, composed in the Society's name by Herr Doctor Georg Wenzky, reads thus:

THE NEKROLOG

CHORUS

O Muses, mute your strings!
Break off, break off your songs of joy! —
to contentment a limit is set —
and sing to comfort afflicted brethren.
Hear what [news] Report brings to you:
hear the lamentations of Leipzig.

It will grieve you:

yet must ye listen.

LEIPZIG

RECITATIVE OR NARRATIVE

The mighty Bach, who to our town —

yea, to the wide realms of Europe —

brought renown, and made little of his powers,

is, alas! a corpse.

The Bach who our Academy

so incomparably adorned:

Bach, who with his delightful wit,

with the sound of his strings

and many kinds of song,

did children, men, and women —

yea, Princes, Kings, and all real connoisseurs —

enchant, teach, and affect:

He has now to trouble our repose;

THE NEKROLOG

he has died, and hasteneth to higher choirs.

ARIOSO

The faithful Bach is dead;

Music and organs are silenced.

O grief, O fall, O misery!

How our hearts bleed!

COMPOSERS OR MUSICIANS

ARIA

Whither hastenest thou, honourable Bach?

Dost thou fill thy guild with bitter woe and anguish?

Ah! shall thy melodies

no more uplift, delight us?
God let thy spirit on thy brethren rest,
that they may help their art to make progress
and magnify His majesty as it deserves.
To all of them we will render praise;
yet follows thee the longing cry:
Whither hastenest thou, honourable Bach?

THE FRIENDS OF MUSIC

NARRATIVE

How skilful, how accomplished
was the transfigured Bach,

so soon from us removed!

  How rich, how individual,

  how unfathomable was

  his noble spirit,

that has delivered itself from mortality!

  How manifold

  was his art,

which did not draw, but dragged to itself

perforce the favour of all connoisseurs!

His flight was high, his warmth of

            [imagination great,

  his praise charming,

his blame caustic.

We ravished heard him magnify the Creator's fame.

His lamentation struck through ears and eyes and hearts:

his rejoicing lightened the heaviest grief.

Alas that we have lost this hero among virtuosos!

   Yet we shall find the more refreshment

   in the masterpieces

   that he has left us

   as a noble relic.

ARIOSO

Jehovah grant long life to the virtuosos

who are yet able to exalt the sweet art!

THE NEKROLOG

THE MUSICAL SOCIETY

TWO-PART ARIA

Wail, brethren, in emulation,
and lament our loss!
Our God has struck the door
so that the strongest pillars quake.
Let the tears run their course,
and therewith

Let the merit of your Bach
be constantly heard in your choirs.
Alas that the oppressed breast
has breath to lament with!

Wail, brethren, in emulation,
and lament our loss!

THE GLORIFIED ONE

NARRATIVE

Lament not, ye friends and connoisseurs;
fortune favours me yet.
Lament not, ye brethren and patrons:
cast but a glance upon these heights!
O could ye hear the beauteous strains
that our choir raises to the glory of God!
O could ye hear the music-making

that here has no ending!
O could ye learn the arts
that my soul has already learnt
since it departed from you!
Ye would take wings and fly
to this summit full of sweetness:
ye would wish my Muse God speed,
not [wish to?] drag it back.
Therefore take comfort
and follow me. What ye have lost in me
ye shall find, and better, within our gates.
Nought, nought is like these singers.

Therefore take comfort.

CHORUS

Ye dwellers in heaven, welcome with joy

the brother who adorned our arts;

and let us with most fervent united voices

sing to the land, honour, and majesty of the Highest!

Who hopes and believes shall enter heaven's gate,

and, glorified, praise God in the angel-choir.

O Christ, help us, then, to do what is needful,

that we also may depart hence in Thy good will.

Ye dwellers in heaven etc.

CANON

APPENDIX I

EXTRACT FROM

Musicalisches | LEXICON | Oder | Musicalische
Bibliothec, | . . . . von Johann Gottfried Wal-
them, 4°. . . . Leipzig, 1732.

BACH (JOH. SEBASTIAN), son of Herr
Joh. Ambrosius Bach, who became a Court
and Town Musician at Eisenach; born
there 21 March 1685; learnt the first principles
of the clavier from his eldest brother Herr
Johann Christoph Bach, who became organist
and a member of the school staff at Ohrdruf;
was organist first in 1703[41] of the New Church
at Arnstadt, and in 1707 of the Church of
St. Blasius, Mühlhausen; came[42] to Weimar in

1708, became here[42] Chamber Musician and
Court Organist, and in 1714 Concertmeister,
to the Duke; in 1717 Capellmeister to the Prince
of Cöthen, and in 1723, after the death of
the late Herr Kuhnau, Director of Music in
Leipzig, and also Capellmeister to the Prince
of Saxe-Weissenfels[43]. Of his admirable
clavier works the following have been published [engraved] on copper: in 1726 a
Partita in B flat major, under the title
'Clavier-Übung, consisting of Preludes,
Allemands, Courantes, Sarabandes, Gigues,

Minuets, etc.' This has been followed by the second [Partita], in C minor, the third, in A minor, the fourth, in D major, the fifth, in G major, and the sixth, in E minor; with which the Opus is probably complete.[44]

The Bach family are probably of Hungarian descent,[45] and all that have borne this name have, so far as is known, been devoted to music; which is perhaps because even the letters b'a'c'h' are melodic when taken in their order — a fact first remarked on by Herr Bach of Leipzig.[46]

APPENDIX II

Extract from

THE BACH GENEALOGY[47]

No.24. Joh. Sebastian Bach, youngest son of Joh. Ambrosius Bach, was born at Eisenach on 21 March 1685. Became (1) Court Musician to Duke Johann Ernst of Weimar, anno 1703. (2) Organist of the New Church at Arnstadt, 1704.[48] (3) Organist of the Church of St. Blasius at Mühlhausen, anno 1707. (4) Chamber[49] and Court Organist at Weimar, anno 1708. (5) At the same Court, anno 1714, Concertmeister also. (6) Capellmeister and

Director of Chamber - music to the Princely
Court of Anhalt - Cöthen, anno 1717. (7) was
called to Leipzig, anno 1723, as Director of
Choral Music and Cantor of St. Thomas'
School ; where according to God's holy Will
he lives yet to the present day, and functions
also as honorary Capellmeister to Weissenfels
and Cöthen.⁵⁰ His family follows { from No.
45 to No. 57. Died 30 July⁵¹ 1750 }

NOTES

THE WORD *CLAVIER* is annoying to the trans-
lator. It means either MANUAL (of an organ
or two-manual harpsichord) or ANY KEY-
BOARD INSTRUMENT, sometimes including
the organ, but not always. Where it has the
latter sense I have left it untranslated, and
the reader must understand harpsichord
(clavicembalo), clavichord, or organ, accord-

ing to the context.

PAGE 2

'These remarks on the persistence of
musical gifts in the Bach family are hardly
exaggerated. At Erfurt the name was so
strongly associated with music that a local
musician would be called a Bach whether
or no that was in fact his name. All Sebastian's
sons were professional musicians, except
Gottfried Heinrich (he was musical, but half-
witted); so was his grandson Wilhelm Friedrich Ernst Bach, who died 25 Dec. 1845, the

last male descendant of Sebastian Bach.

² From the Genealogy we learn that Veit Bach was a miller. The author of the Genealogy evidently knew nothing of his life before he left Hungary, and probably thought he was born there ; in some such way arose, no doubt , the notion that the family was of Hungarian origin (see Appendix I). Actually, the name Bach is recorded in Thuringia from 1509 onwards. Terry suggests that Veit was born at Wechmar (the church there is dedicated to St. Vitus) and

wandered to Hungary in his youth.

At any rate, when he left Hungary (probably
during the reign of the counter-Reformationist
Rudolf II, 1576-1612) it was in Wechmar that
he settled; and he died there 8 Mar. 1619. The
Genealogy says, 'His greatest delight was a
little zither, which he would take with him into
the mill and play as the wheel went round.
(It must have sounded well, the two of them!
However, he thus taught himself to keep time.)
And this, it seems, was the beginning of the
musical gifts of his descendants.'

PAGE 6

[3] To judge from the organ chorale-preludes in Keller's collection of ancient works (Peters edition) two of these five parts must have been supplied by the imagination of Christoph's audiences.

PAGE 8

[4] For further information about the early Bachs see Grove and the major works on Sebastian.

[5] The Nekrolog, Walther, and the Genealogy agree on this date. It is Old Style. The Eisenach

registers (facsimile in H. Reimann, Johann Sebastian Bach, Zweite Auflage, . . . erweitert
von Bruno Schrader. Berlin [1921]) do not record
Bach's birth, but only his baptism on March
23 : two days later, as the custom was.

[6] Ambrosius was born 22 Feb. 1645, and died
31 Jan 1695. He married Elisabeth Lämmerhirt,
daughter of a furrier, on 8 Ap. 1668. Elisabeth
was born 24 Feb. 1644, and died 3 May 1694.

[7] This Christoph died in 1693.

PAGE 9

[8] Christoph was born in 1671. He had received lessons from the well-known organist and composer Johann Pachelbel, who stood godfather to his sister Johanna Juditha Bach, born in 1680.

PAGE 12

[9] Emanuel and Agricola evidently thought that Christoph died in 1699 or 1700. Actually he lived until 1721.

PAGE 13

[10] The words 'In the year 1700' are a correction.

The original has 'After his brother's death'.
See note 9.

Since Sebastian's arrival in Ohrdruf in
1695, Christoph had had two or three children
born to him; and it would seem that by 1700
there was no room in the house for Sebastian.
The Ohrdruf school register records that Bach
left on 15 Mar. 1700 'ob defectum hospitiorum'.
There is a precisely similar entry concerning
Erdmann on 19 Jan. 1700.

Lüneburg was a long way off, and the boys
must have had some reason for going there; it

is reasonable to suppose that they were recom-
mended to the authorities at Lüneburg by one
Elias Herder, who had been educated there
before coming to ~~Lüneburg~~ Ohrdruf as a master
in 1697. Both boys were at Lüneburg for Easter
1700 (April 3).

Erdmann and Bach kept in touch until
1730 at least; in that year Bach sent to his
old schoolfellow an important letter that will
be referred to later.

PAGE 14

"Little is known of Bach's schooldays apart

from the account given here. From the registers
of both schools it can be deduced that he made
good progress in his studies; he received a
sound general education, including Latin.

The well-known anecdote of Bach's finding
money in two herring-heads, which fell at his
feet as he sat sniffing hungrily outside a
wayside hostelry (Marpurg, Legende einiger
Musikheiligen, 1786), refers to one of these
journeys to Hamburg.

Hamburg was thirty miles from Lüneburg,
Celle sixty. The Nekrolog is too much concerned

with Bach's 'unheard-of zeal for study', and
the long journeys he accordingly undertook
in order to hear Reinken and the band at
Celle, to mention Georg Böhm, who was on
his doorstep at St. John's, Lüneburg. Böhm
was a Thuringian and a pupil of Reinken's.
His characteristic style seems to be reflected in
Bach's early Chorale-Partitas and certain
other works.

PAGE 15

[12] It must have been at this time that Bach
competed for the organistship of the Market Church,

Sangerhausen. This post fell vacant in 1702
(July 3). In 1736 another vacancy occurred;
and Bach wrote to one J. F. Klemm, a Councillor at Sangerhausen, recommending his son
Johann Gottfried Bernhard for the post (see
note 25). In his second letter to Klemm, dated
18 Nov. 1736, Bach refers to his having been a
candidate for the same post thirty years before,
and having 'obtained the vote', although 'the
higher powers' caused another candidate to
be appointed. 'The higher powers' must have
been the Duke of Weissenfels, lord of the town;

the successful candidate was one Kobelius, whose grandfather had been Court Organist at Weissenfels. The courts of Weissenfels and Weimar were on friendly terms; Bach's appointment to Weimar may have been arranged as a compensation for his failure at Sangerhausen. However this may be, Easter Day (April 8) 1703 found him installed in the chamber orchestra maintained by Duke Johann Ernst of Weimar.

This Duke is not to be confused with his elder brother, whom Bach served from 1708 to 1717. See note 22, p. 113.

PAGE 15

[13] On 7 Aug. 1581, a very hot day, one Hans
Nebel of Arnstadt saw fit to tar his roof. A
neighbour who pointed out the danger of fire
was told to go to the devil; whereupon the latter
did his stuff. The ensuing conflagration involved the church of St. Boniface, which was
not rebuilt until 1676-83.

The organ, naturally, was newer than the
church. It was not finished until the beginning of July 1703; and was then examined
by experts, of whom Bach (aged 18) was one.

His expenses were paid on July 13, and in the
document concerning this payment he is
referred to as Court Organist to the Duke of
Weimar. In reality, one Effler seems to have
held that post; but it may be supposed that
Bach, officially a string-player in Duke Johann
Ernst's band, had played upon the organ
in the chapel attached to the Court of the
reigning Duke, Wilhelm Ernst. In any case,
it is clear that he already had a reputation as
an organist.

Bach opened the organ, presumably on one

of the Sundays in July.' The minute of his
appointment as organist is dated 9 Aug. 1703;
his formal induction (durch Handschlag)
took place on Aug. 14.

The words 'Later in the same year' are a
correction. The Nekrolog reads 'Das Jahr drauf'
(In the following year), thus dating the appointment
1704, as the Genealogy does expressly.

PAGE 16

'4 The subject of the Passacaglia is said to
owe something to one André Raison. There is
an article on Bach's borrowings from the French

in the Bach-Jahrbuch for 1910.

[15] This was in October 1705. The distance is
300 miles; it is not surprising that Bach over-
stayed his leave and consequently fell into
trouble with his pastors and masters. The latter
undoubtedly had just cause for complaint,
quite apart from his late return on this occasion.
Bach had a hasty temper, it would seem; he was
an indifferent organizer, and at no time did he
show any sympathy with the unmusical. He therefore made a poor choirmaster. In addition, his

extemporized preludes to the hymn-verses failed
to give satisfaction; it was said that they had
been too long, and their harmony extravagant,
and that when he was asked to shorten and
simplify them, he promptly made them too short.
(He was a true organist! One is reminded of
Samuel Sebastian Wesley, of whom it is said
that he was sacked by one of those Deans with
whom he was perpetually at war, but reinstated
by the Bishop; whereupon he played for his
next voluntary 'Fixed in His everlasting seat'.)
Finally, he was questioned about his introducing

'a stranger maiden' into the church. It is supposed that this was Maria Barbara Bach, his
cousin and first wife, and that he brought her
to the church to sing to his accompaniment
(not, of course, at services).

At Arnstadt Bach wrote the 'Capriccio on
the Departure of his beloved Brother', a piece
of programme music (for clavier) modelled
on the Biblical Sonatas of Kuhnau (David
and Goliath, etc.), and inspired by his brother
Johann Jakob's removal to Sweden in 1704.

Terry gives a photograph and a careful

specification of the Arnstadt organ, whose
console is still in existence. The pedalboard
had a compass extending from CC to d', but
lacking CC sharp : an arrangement not
unusual at that date.

[16] Bach was appointed on 15 June 1707, and
probably began his duties on Sept. 15. At
Mühlhausen he married for the first time; see
p. 38. Here also he drew up a specification of
the work to be done on his organ, which was to
be rebuilt. Much has been made of his inclusion

of a pedal glockenspiel and of his demand that
the tremulant should be put in order ; it has
not been so much emphasized that the glockenspiel was asked for and paid for by the parish-
ioners, and that the tremulant had to be put
right whether Bach intended to use it or not.

The glockenspiel was to have had twenty-
six bells. This gives us the compass of the
pedal-board : CC to d', without CC sharp,
as at Arnstadt.

The rebuilding of the organ was not completed until 1709, after Bach's removal to

Weimar; but he gave the opening recital. This
apparently took place on the Reformation Festival, an occasion for which the chorale 'Ein'
feste Burg' was appropriate. Bach's solitary
prelude on this chorale was copied by J.G.
Walther, who marked registration such as Bach
might have used at Mühlhausen to show off
the new stops he had specified; and it may be
supposed that he played the prelude on that
occasion. Whether he composed it specially, or
was merely using an old favourite of the congregation's, is unknown.

PAGE 17

7 Bach's letter of resignation is dated 25 June 1708. In it he speaks of his not having been allowed to do his work without opposition from his own congregation, and says that this opposition shows no sign of abating. It is possible, too, that he became involved in a theological controversy that was then agitating the town.

His exact position at Weimar when he first went there is not known. In the above-mentioned letter he refers to his appointment to the 'Hof Capelle und Cammer Music' (as Terry puts it, to 'the Duke's general musical establishment and the select body of string players who performed in his private apartments'.) In the Genealogy he is described as 'Cammer und Hoforganist in Weimar, An. 1708'. Walther says he was at first 'Cammer-Musicus und Hof-Organist'. Certainly he was Court Organist by 1710; in the financial year Michaelmas 1710–Michaelmas 1711 he received an allowance for the heating of the organ chamber in the Court chapel. There is no record of what happened to his predecessor Johann Effler. Most probably

Bach took over the organist's duties as soon
as he arrived.

The specification of the organ is given in
Gottfried Albin Wette's 'Historische Nach-
richten von der berühmten Residenz-Stadt Weimar'
(Weimar, 1737). If I remember rightly, Wette
includes a glockenspiel, which is omitted from
Terry's quotation (p.97 of the Biography). But
I may be quite wrong. In any case, the glockenspiel was added between Michaelmas 1715
and 1716; and this is the most satisfactory piece
of evidence for Bach's reputed interest in these

devices — so far as I have been able to discover.

About this time Bach seems to have had access to an organ with an e' pedalboard, though he did not use that note frequently. It will be found in the Fugue à la Gigue, the early Prelude and Fugue in G, the Prelude and Fugue in A, and the Second Concerto. The last-named work was almost certainly produced at Weimar, before the death (in 1715) of the young Duke Johann Ernst, for whom Walther made a number of similar arrangements.[x] I suspect,

[x] Bach's four Concertos are not original works.

therefore, that the organ for which Bach wrote
these high pedal parts was either his own or
that in the Town Church, where Walther was
organist ; unless, indeed, these works were composed for a pedal harpsichord, which seems
unlikely.

[18] There is no reason to question the Nekrolog's
statement that Bach composed most of his organ
works at Weimar; but a reservation must be
made : the works as we know them may be
products of elaborate later revision. For instance,

the early versions of the Eighteen Chorale-preludes
probably date from Weimar; but the revised
versions familiar to us were made after 1730.

PAGE 18

[19] The appointment dates from Mar. 2; and
one of the duties was to produce new Cantatas
monthly.

PAGE 19

[20] F. W. Zachau, Handel's master, died in Aug.
1712. Bach visited Halle late in 1713, and was
perhaps attracted by the organ then under construction in the Markt- or Liebfrauenkirche.

The post being vacant, he performed a 'test-
piece' there — probably Cantata 21. He returned
to Weimar, where he received an invitation to
Halle (the letter is dated Dec. 14). Bach was not
altogether satisfied with the conditions of the
appointment; and what with this and the Duke's
unwillingness to let him go, it would seem that
the matter remained unsettled until Bach's
appointment as Concertmeister at Weimar
(Mar. 2, 1714) caused him to refuse the Halle
post. Some of the correspondence has been lost;
but from Bach's letter of March 19 it is evident

that he had been accused of using the invitation
to Halle as a means of extorting promotion at
Weimar.

At some unknown date between Michaelmas
1714 and Michaelmas 1715 Bach had an
accident for which he received twelve florins
compensation. In 1714 (perhaps during his
convalescence? but it seems unlikely) he
found leisure for the lengthy task of copying
Frescobaldi's 'Fiori musicali' — 104 pages
of MS.

It would seem that it was late in 1714

(after Sept. 7) that Bach visited Cassel for some unknown reason and received from the Hereditary Prince Friedrich a ring, as reward for his virtuosity on the pedals. 'His feet, flying over the pedals as though they were winged, made the notes reverberate like thunder in a storm,' wrote Constantin Bellermann, continuing: 'if Bach's skilful feet deserved such a bounty, what gift must the Prince have offered to reward his hands as well?' (Programma in quo Parnassus Musarum, etc. (1743); tr. Terry. See also Adlung's Anleitung (1758), p. 690: and

an article by Carl Scherer in Monats. f. Musik.
geschichte, Jahrg. 25, p. 129.)

At Weimar Bach was intimate with J. G.
Walther (p. 219), and presumably made the
acquaintance of J. M. Gesner, who became
Conrector at the Gymnasium in 1715. They
met again at Leipzig in 1730.

In 1716 Bach attended his master on a
visit to Weissenfels, and performed his secular
Cantata 'Was mir behagt' there on the Duke's
birthday (Feb. 23). Shortly afterwards (Ap. 20)
he was invited to report on the new organ at

Halle that had (perhaps) attracted him two
years before. The examination took place on
April 29 and 30; and on Sunday May 3 the
organ was opened. A banquet followed, whose
appalling menu (still preserved) justifies Terry's
remark: 'Little wonder that a big blot fell on
the 'Bach' as the writer signed a receipt for
six thalers, his fee!'

PAGE 24

[21] Marchand was born in 1669 and died in
1732. There are several accounts of the contest,
which differ a good deal in detail. It seems

curious, to say the least of it, that Bach should have been specially invited to Dresden by Jean-Baptiste Volumier (obviously a Frenchman) in order to discredit another Frenchman; and perhaps Terry is right in suggesting that Bach visited Dresden in order to hear Marchand, the contest being arranged afterwards. It took place about September. There is no evidence that Bach was deprived of a present from the King, or even that any such present was ever spoken of.

22 The story of Bach's removal to Cöthen begins with his relations with the Dukes of Weimar.

When he first went to Weimar in 1703, it was to serve Duke Johann Ernst. In 1708 his employer was Duke Wilhelm Ernst, elder brother of Johann, who, meanwhile, had died in 1707. The brothers had been on bad terms.

Wilhelm was childless; Johann had two sons, Ernst August and Johann Ernst. The former came of age in 1709, and got on with his uncle no better than his father had done. He was a pupil of Bach's, as was also his brother Johann Ernst the younger,

who died in 1715; and Bach was evidently on
intimate terms with this side of the family, for
Ernst August's wife stood godmother to a
short-lived son of Bach's born at Cöthen in
1718.

    In Bach's last years at Weimar relations
between Wilhelm Ernst and Ernst August
became so bad that the former forbade members
of his Capelle (among others) to visit his nephew's
court. Bach must have found the situation
difficult. Further, on 1 Dec. 1716 the senile
Capellmeister at Weimar (one Drese) died;

and Bach had reason to be annoyed when the
vacancy was filled by Drese's son, who does not
seem to have been particularly competent, instead
of by himself, who since his appointment as
Concertmeister in March 1714 had been fulfilling
one of the Capellmeister's most important duties:
the composition of Cantatas (monthly).

    On 24 Jan. 1716 Ernst August had married
Eleonore, sister of Prince Leopold of Anhalt-Cöthen;
and it was, no doubt, as a result of Bach's
intimacy with his sister's husband that Leopold
offered him the Capellmeistership at Cöthen. He

accepted, and was formally appointed on 5 Aug.
1717; but Wilhelm Ernst refused to allow him
to go; no doubt he was incensed by Bach's
intimacy with his nephew, and by that nephew's
(presumable) assistance in obtaining Bach
his new post. After the contest with Marchand
Bach probably felt that now was the time to
press for his release; at all events, he did so,
to such purpose that on Nov. 6 he was im-
prisoned for his obstinacy. He was released on
Dec. 2 'with a grudging permission,' says the
Court Secretary, 'to retire from the Duke's service.'

(Emanuel and Agricola perhaps thought it as
well to draw a decent veil over this incident.)
By Dec. 10 he was settled in Cöthen; his family
may have moved in before that date.

    With his departure from Weimar Bach ceased
to be a professional organist. At Cöthen it was
not his duty to play at all, but to conduct and
provide music for the Prince's band. On what
organ he kept up his technique we do not know.
There were three available: in the Schloss chapel
a two-manual of thirteen stops (the Prince did
not maintain an organist of his own; he was

a Calvinist, and no elaborate music was performed in his chapel): at St. James' (also a
Calvinist church) a fairly large organ : and at
St. Agnes' a small organ with an f' sharp
pedalboard — for which there is no particular
reason to suppose that the Orgelbüchlein preludes
on 'Gottes Sohn' and 'In dulci jubilo' were
originally composed.

According to Bach, Prince Leopold (born in
1694) 'loved and understood music' (letter
to Erdmann). Certainly he seems to have been
much attached to his gifted Capellmeister, whose
salary

he made equal to that of the Hofmarschall, the
second highest of the Court functionaries.

Bach had hardly arrived in Cöthen when he
was invited to Leipzig to examine a new organ
by Johann Scheibe, in St. Paul's Church. His
report is dated 17 Dec. 1717. There is reason to
believe that while in Leipzig he performed
Cantata 61, at either St. Thomas' or St. Nicholas'
(the cantata had had its first performance at
Weimar in 1714).

In May 1718 Bach, with five other members
of the Capelle and a clavicembalo, accompanied

Leopold to Carlsbad. They were back in Cöthen
by June. On Nov. 17 the Prince and his younger
brother stood godfathers to the last of Bach's
children by his first wife (Leopold Augustus,
b. 15 Nov.; buried 28 Sept. 1719). It was this
child to whom Leopold's sister the Duchess
Eleonore stood godmother.

In May 1720 Bach again visited Carlsbad
with the Prince. They returned in July to find
Maria Barbara dead and already buried
(p. 40).

PAGE 25

[23] So the Nekrolog. The year was 1720, and the month (probably) October. The circumstances of Bach's visit are obscure; but Terry is perhaps right in supposing that he went there to inquire about the vacancy at St. James' caused by the death of Heinrich Friese on 12 Sept. 1720. On 21 Nov. the church authorities decided to invite eight men to compete for the post on Nov. 28; Bach was one of those named. Leopold's birthday fell on Nov. 29; and as musical celebrations were expected, Bach would have been unable

to remain in Hamburg for the competition. Further-
more, it was a rule, and well known, that the
successful candidate would be expected to con-
tribute to the church funds; and this may have
deterred him. He played to Reinken (1623–
1722), no doubt; but for the presence of 'the
Magistracy and many other notables' we have
only the Nekrolog's evidence.

The 'Great' G minor and the two preludes
on 'An Wasserflüssen Babylon' are commonly
associated with this occasion.

The successful candidate was one Heitmann;

his appointment cost him 4000 marks. The
pastor, Erdmann Neumeister (a well-known
compiler of Cantata libretti, some of which
were used by Bach) had perhaps hoped that
Bach would be appointed; and shortly afterwards, in a sermon on the Christmas gospel,
he said that if an angel from heaven had
competed for the post, he would have been rejected
unless he had brought money with him (Mattheson,
Der musicalische Patriot, Hamburg 1728, p. 316).

On 24 March 1721 Bach wrote the dedicatory
note of the Brandenburg Concertos, from which

it is evident that these works had been commissioned 'two years ago'; it does not appear
that they were either acknowledged or performed.
Bach's second marriage took place on 3 Dec.
1721 (p. 40). Eight days later (Dec. 11) Leopold,
in whose service Bach had expected to end his
days, married (in Bach's words) 'a Bernburg
wife, and in consequence, as it seemed, his
musical inclination abated, while his new
Princess proved to be an amusa. So it pleased
God to call me here [Leipzig] as director Musices and Cantor of the Thomasschule. At

first I found it not altogether agreeable to
become a simple Cantor after having been a
Capellmeister, and for that reason I forbore
from coming to a *resolution* for three months.
However, I received such *favorable* reports
of the *situation*, that, having particularly in
mind my sons' *studia*, and after invoking
divine guidance, I at last made up my mind,
came to Leipzig, performed my Probe, and
received the post' (letter to Erdmann, tr.
Terry. Italics — the underlining — indicate
non-German words).

PAGE 27

[24] Johann Kuhnau, Cantor of the Thomas-schule since 1701, died on 5 June 1722. Of the six candidates for the vacancy who were under consideration on July 14, by far the most notable was G.P. Telemann (one of Emanuel Bach's godfathers); he was offered the post, and accepted. Things had gone so far by Aug. 14. Telemann, however, simply made use of his appointment to extort an increase of salary from his employers at Hamburg; and about the end of October he refused the Cantorate.

Bach did not appear as a candidate until between Nov. 23 and Dec. 21; of the five men under consideration on the latter date, he and Graupner (of Darmstadt) were regarded as the most hopeful; and the latter was preferred. He was in charge of the music from Christmas until mid-January, and would have been appointed had not his master increased his salary. In the end he withdrew, in a letter dated 23 March 1723. Meanwhile Bach had performed Cantata 22 as his test-piece on Feb.7 (Quinquagesima); and, pre-

sumably because no-one else was available, he
was responsible for the Passion Music at St.
Thomas' on Good Friday, March 26. So the
St. John Passion had its first performance.

On April 4 Prince Leopold's wife died – too
late. The Leipzig Council considered Graupner's
withdrawal on April 9; Bach obtained his
release from Cöthen on the 13th; and on the
22nd his appointment was agreed upon.
On May 5 he signed a bond defining his
duties; on the 30th he performed Cantata 75;
and on June 1 he was formally inducted to

TO PAGE 27   129

the school. There he remained until his death
twenty-seven years later.

One thinks of Bach as an organist; and
it is curious to find that that was his profession
for fourteen years only (1703-1717). After his
six years' dalliance with secular music at
Cöthen, he returned to the Church indeed, and
for good; but not as an organist. His pastors
and masters expected him to compose and conduct music for the churches of St. Thomas and
St. Nicholas, to train his choirs, and in addition
to teach non-musical subjects in the school,

perform sundry disciplinary duties, and generally do what he was told. They got more (or
perhaps it would be more correct to say, less) than
they expected. Bach soon chose for his favourite
title 'Director Musices'; and on composition
and 'direction' (conducting) he concentrated;
school duties and even choir-training were
tasks that he found irksome, and he fairly
soon found (legitimate) means of evading
them. This does not mean that he was lazy.
There is no reason to disbelieve the Nekrolog's
statement (p.36) that he composed five cycles

of Cantatas for the Sundays and festivals of
the ecclesiastical year : 295 in all. Of these
he had composed about thirty before he went
to Leipzig ; the rest were produced between
1723 and about 1744 — on the average, about
one a month (cf. his duties as Concertmeister
at Weimar, note 19, p. 106).

It was not long before the Leipzig authorities
had a taste of the new Cantor's quality :   For
instrumentalists (it must be remembered that
the weekly Cantatas had orchestral accompani-
ments) the Cantors had to depend on what they

could pick up from various sources; in particular,
from among the University students. The University had a church of its own — St. Paul's;
before 1710, regular services were not held there,
but the occasional festival services were taken
by Kuhnau. This duty was known as the Old
Service; and for performing it Kuhnau received
a small salary. But in 1710 regular Sunday
services were begun. The University authorities
did not wish it to be thought that S.Paul's went
with the Cantorate of St. Thomas' of necessity;
and Kuhnau was only able to retain office,

and with it his valuable connection with the
student-instrumentalists, by undertaking to
be responsible for the Sunday services (the
'New Service') as well as for the Old Service,
without any increase in his salary. When Telemann was appointed Cantor in 1722 he obtained the University post as well; but he was
plainly told that he received it on his merits,
and not simply because he was Cantor of St.
Thomas'.

During the interregnum that followed Kuhnau's death the duties at St. Paul's were per-

formed by the organist of St. Nicholas', Johann
Gottlieb Görner. When it became evident that
there was a chance of Graupner's not being
released from Darmstadt, Görner applied to
be formally appointed; and on 3 April 1723
he became responsible for both Old and New
Services. (Bach's appointment to St. Thomas'
was agreed upon on the 22nd.)

At Michaelmas 1723 Bach demanded
the salary due to him for the Old Service. (Of
course, he had not performed these duties; he
was merely asserting his right, as Cantor, to

direct the Old Service. He maintained that the
University had had no business to attempt to
break in 1710, the old-established association.)
After some argument it was agreed that the
post was his; but it was not until later that he
contrived to extort from the authorities even half
his proper salary; and even after two years of
controversy he could get no further. Accordingly,
he appealed to the King (Augustus II, Elector
of Saxony). After investigation the Elector gave
his decision (21 Jan. 1726): Bach was to be
responsible for the Old Service, and to receive

the proper salary; the New Service was at the University's disposal. No provision was made for such non-recurrent occasions as public mournings; whence arose further trouble in 1727 (see below, p.139; further details in B.J.1925).

Meanwhile, on 2 Nov. 1723 Bach had taken his choir to Störmthal to open an organ by Zacharias Hildebrand; and at Vespers on Christmas Day ne performed the Latin Magnificat.

For the Passion Music of 1724 Bach repeated the St. John. It was customary that a work should

have its first performance at St. Thomas', but be
repeated the following year at St. Nicholas'. Bach
found the conditions at the latter church un-
satisfactory, and issued programmes announcing
a performance at St. Thomas'; but the Council
agreed to repair St. Nicholas' clavier and adapt
the choir gallery to his requirements, so he re-
called his programmes.

On 25 June 1724 Bach, described as 'der
berühmter Cantor und Capellmeister', opened
a new organ at the church of St. Johannes and
St. Salvator, Gera. In July, (1724) and again in Dec.

1725, he and his wife were paid for visits to
Cöthen. It was in 1725 that Bach first set
texts by 'Picander' (Christian Friedrich Hen-
rici), a facile hack-writer whose rather taste-
less productions frequently served Bach in
later years.

A funeral on 4 Feb. 1726 was probably the
occasion for which the magnificent motet 'Be
not afraid' was composed. This year also
saw the appearance of the first Partita, engraved
and published 'in Verlegung des Autoris'; it
was dedicated to the short-lived infant son of

Prince Leopold, who had married for the second time in 1725. Nov. 30 was the new Princess' birthday; and Bach visited Cöthen to perform the cantata 'Steigt freudig in die Luft' in her honour.

On 6 Sept. 1727 the wife of the Elector died, and Saxony went into mourning for four months. Hans von Kirchbach, a young nobleman studying at the University, arranged for the delivery (by himself) of a funeral Oration in St. Paul's, with accompanying music which he commissioned Bach to write. The University students had already

given Bach, rather than Görner, one or two
commissions for semi-official functions organ-
ized by themselves; but the Oration was to
be a formal University affair; and as the
Elector's decision of 1726 took no account of
such occasions, Görner thought it worth his
while to assert his claim to compose the music
— and receive the fee.

The Oration was to take place on Oct. 17.
On the 9th the University authorities told Kirchbach that Bach must take no part in the
ceremony. Kirchbach replied that it was too

late; Bach had been paid, and had already
written some of the music. Then the University
said that Bach might compose the music, but
Görner must perform it. Kirchbach took no
notice of this. On Oct. 11 Görner told the Council
that he must know where he stood. They sent
immediately to Kirchbach, repeating their former
message in peremptory terms. Kirchbach said at
first that if he were further pestered he would
cancel the whole thing; but later agreed to meet
Görner, and in the end offered him twelve
thalers to stand down. Görner accepted; but

produced a document to be signed by Bach,
binding the latter to keep out of any such cere-
monies in the future. Next day (Oct. 12) the
University Clerk took the document to Bach for
his signature; his report was, 'I did my best
from 11 to 12, but without success.' Bach never
did sign. He finished the music on the 15th, and
on the 17th conducted it, 'fixed in his everlasting
seat' at the clavier in the gallery (B.J. 1925;
Bitter ii,9 and Sicul, Das thränende Leipzig,
1727).

In 1728 there was a minor controversy, which

seems to have been decided in Bach's favour, about his right to choose the hymns before and after the sermon.

PAGE 27

[25] Leopold died 19 Nov. 1728; Bach's Trauer-Music was performed at Cöthen on 24 March 1729. Part of this work, which has been lost, consisted of movements from the St. Matthew Passion fitted to new words by Picander.

The Passion itself had its first performance on Good Friday (April 15) 1729. Gerber, a pupil of Bach's, wrote (three years later): 'Some high

officials and well-born ladies in one of the gal-
leries began to sing the first Chorale with great
devotion from their books. But as the theatrical
music proceeded, they were thrown into the greatest wonderment, saying to each other, "What
does it all mean?" while one old lady, a widow,
exclaimed, "God help us! 'tis surely an Opera-
comedy!"' (Bitter ii, 58; tr. Terry.)

On 16 Oct. 1729 Johann Heinrich Ernesti,
Rector of the Thomasschule, died. He had been
Rector since 1684, and thus must have been an
old man at his death; I cannot at present

find the date of his birth. In his later years he
had grown slack, and the school had suffered
accordingly; but Bach and he had been on
good terms: his wife and daughter had stood
as godmothers to two of Bach's children. For the
memorial service Bach wrote the motet 'Der Geist
hilft unser Schwachheit auf'.

The new Rector was not appointed until 8 June
1730; the choice was a fortunate one for Bach —
Johann Matthias Gesner, who had probably
known Bach at Weimar (p. 110), and greatly
admired him. In his edition of Quintilian's

'Institutiones Oratoriae' Gesner comments at
length on his author's remarks about a lyre-
player, concluding ' I'm an honest admirer
of your ancient world, but I tell you this Bach
of mine, or another, if you can find one like
him, is worth any number of Orpheuses, and
twenty singers like Arion.'

How far Bach's contemporaries were able
to appreciate his compositions is made all too
clear by the widow's opinion of the St. Matthew
Passion, quoted above; and the Leipzig Council
—made up, no doubt, like other such bodies,

of persons even less musical than that horrified
old lady — saw in the change of Rector an
opportunity of getting rid of their troublesome
Cantor. At a meeting on 2 Aug. 1730 they complained of his frequent absences from Leipzig
(under the bond he had signed in 1723 he was
supposed to ask permission whenever he wished
to leave the town; but apparently he never did);
and Hofrath Adrian Steger summed up by
saying that the Cantor 'does nothing, refuses
to explain his conduct, and neglects his
singing lessons, not to mention other instances

of his unsatisfactoriness.' Syndicus Job added
that Bach was 'incorrigible'; and they decided
to stop his salary.

This did not so affect what Bach called his
'accidentia' — the fees for funerals and weddings
that made up the greater part of his income; but,
needless to say, it stirred him to action. He retorted
in a letter dated Aug. 23, maintaining (in lan-
guage whose extreme simplicity shows exactly
what he thought of the Council) that the faults of
his choir and orchestra were due not to him, but
to the admission into the school (against his

recommendation) of unmusical boys, to the disappearance of 'the occasional *beneficia* which used to find their way into the pockets of 'the University student-instrumentalists (from whom the orchestra was to a large extent recruited), and to other causes beyond his control.

The Council did nothing more; and Bach ignored them, except that on 28 Oct. 1730 he wrote that important letter to Erdmann which has been previously referred to. He wrote: '(1) this situation is not as good as it was represented

to be, (2) various *accidentia* relative to my
station have been withdrawn, (3) living is expensive, and (4) my masters are strange folk
with very little care for music in them. Consequently, I am subjected to constant annoyance, jealousy, and persecution. It is therefore
in my mind, with God's assistance, to seek my
fortune elsewhere. If your Honour [his school-
mate!] knows of or should hear of a *convenable*
station in your town [Danzig], I beg you to let
me have your valuable *recommendation*.' He
goes on to give details of his present income:

'if the death-rate is higher than <u>ordinairement</u>, my <u>accidentia</u> increase in <u>proportion</u>; but Leipzig is a healthy place, and for the past year, as it happens, I have received about 100 Kronen [one seventh of his total income] less than usual in funeral <u>accidentia</u>.'

Nothing came of this letter. Gesner was already in office; and he soon took care to make Bach's life easier, in more ways than one. At the reopening of the school (5 June 1732) after its enlargement, new rules were issued, in which Gesner's interest in the musical side of the school's work is made evident.

Forkel or somebody has recorded Bach's taking his eldest son, Wilhelm Friedemann, to the opera in Dresden; he would say, 'Shall we go and hear the pretty tunes?', or words to that effect. He was apparently friendly with J. A. Hasse, Capellmeister to the Electoral Court at Dresden; and was present at the first performance of Hasse's opera 'Cleofide' (13 Sept. 1731. See M. Falck, Wilhelm Friedemann Bach (1919), p. 12). Next day he gave a recital at St. Sophia's, in the presence of Hasse and other personages.

His playing inspired some quasi-poetry (Bitter,
ii, 157, and Terry, 211). It was seven years since
his last recital, so far as we know (B.J. 1925, p. 93);
but now in February 1732 he played at Stöntzsch
(Neue Sächsische Kirchengalerie, Bd. XV. Die
Ephorie Borna. Hrsg. von den Geistlichen der
Ephorie, p. 1091); and in Sept. 1732 he revisited
Cassel, to report on the enlarged organ in St.
Martin's. He and Anna Magdalena arrived
on 21 Sept. 1732, and the organ was opened on
Sunday the 28th (authorities given in Terry's
footnotes to pp. 211-2).

On 1 Feb. 1733 the Elector died, and Saxony
went into mourning until July. This meant that
no Cantatas were required for the churches, and
Bach had leisure for another occupation. That
he liked the title of Capellmeister is evident from
his letter to Erdmann (p. 125); and not only did
he value a Court appointment for its own sake:
he also thought (see below) that it might serve
to protect him against the 'annoyance, jealousy,
and persecution' that beset him at Leipzig. As
the post of Electoral Capellmeister was held by
his friend Hasse, he decided to try to obtain

an appointment as Court Composer; and as the
Elector was a Roman Catholic, and a secular
work perhaps seemed an inappropriate offering
during a period of public mourning, he chose
to make his diploma-piece a setting of the Kyrie
and Gloria (the Lutheran Missa) — texts common
to Catholics and Lutherans. This was the beginning of the B minor Mass.

The Missa was finished by the summer of
1733. In June the post of organist at St. Sophia's,
Dresden, fell vacant; and on the 7th Bach drafted
an application on behalf of his son Friedemann.

The latter was heard on June 22, and appointed forthwith. He received the organ key on July 11, examined the organ, and began his duties on Aug. 1. Bach must have stayed with him in Dresden for at least part of this time; for the dedicatory letter that accompanied the Missa to the Court is addressed from Dresden and dated July 27. In this letter Bach speaks of his having been 'constantly exposed to undeserved affronts, even the confiscation of the _accidentia_ due to me, annoyances not likely to recur should your Majesty be pleased to admit me to your Capella.'

Unfortunately for Bach, the Elector was at this time much concerned with the situation in Poland, where a Nationalist movement, not quelled until the summer of 1734, was on foot. He turned a deaf ear not only to Bach's petition, but also to the series of congratulatory works that Bach and his Collegium Musicum performed in Leipzig on 3 Aug. 1733, his birthday: 5 September, his son's birthday: 8 December, the birthday of the Queen-Electress: 17 Jan. 1734, the coronation of the Elector and his Queen at Cracow: 3 August, his birthday: 5

October, the anniversary of his election to the
throne of Poland (next day died Gottfried
Reiche, trumpeter, of a stroke attributed to his
exertions on the previous evening in an atmos
sphere of torch-smoke): and 7 October, his
birthday (I have followed Terry, although he
seems to give the Elector two birthdays). The
works produced on these occasions were for
the most part adaptations of material already
available, including the Hosanna of the Mass
(5 Oct. 1734) and parts of the Christmas Oratorio,
which latter was performed as a whole in 1734.

Bach's intensive cultivation of his sovereign ceased with the cantata performed on 7 Oct. 1734; and we hear no more of his Court appointment until 1736.

In 1734 he may have visited Cöthen to inspect the St. Agnus organ, which had been enlarged (B.J. 1925, p. 95); and this year Philipp Emanuel left home to become a student at Frankfurt. This year also, Gesner left Leipzig; and a new Rector, Johann August Ernesti, was installed on Nov. 18.

Ernesti had been Conrector since 1731, and

was at this time on friendly terms with Bach;
he was godfather to Bach's sons Johann August
and Johann Christian on 5 Nov. 1733 and 7
Sept. 1735 respectively. But Ernesti, only 27
when he became Rector, belonged to a later
generation than Bach and Gesner; and he
held the view of his contemporaries, that the
musical obligations of schools such as St.
Thomas' stood in the way of their efficiency
as educational agencies. With on the one hand
a young and tactless man holding such views,
and on the other hand Bach's pugnacious and

obstinate temper, the train was laid ; the necessary
spark was duly supplied in 1736 .

Meanwhile the organist of St. Mary's, Mühlhausen, died on 6 April 1735 ; Bach wrote two
letters to the Council recommending his son Johann
Gottfried Bernhard (b. 11 May 1715) for the post.
Father and son went to Mühlhausen for the
competition, in which Bernhard was successful;
he was appointed on June 16 (Mühlhäuser Gesch-
ichtsblätter, Jahrg. xxi, 1920–1, p. 71). Bach must
have felt the departure of his three gifted sons,
with whose aid he had in former years been able

to 'arrange a concert vocaliter and instrument-
aliter' (letter to Erdmann).

In 1736 came the inevitable quarrel with
Ernesti. This year one Gottfried Theodor Krause
was about to leave the Thomasschule for the
University. He was senior prefect; and as such
he, like the other prefects, had not only to maintain discipline but also to act as conductor at
services and parts of services that were not held
to require the presence of the Cantor himself.
He had been authorized by Bach to punish
offenders, if necessary, on his own account;

so on one occasion he caned a boy for bad
conduct at a wedding. The boy said that Krause
had made his back bleed (although the school
hairdresser found 'not the slightest trace' of any
such thing); and complained to Ernesti, who
ordered Krause, a young man of twenty-two,
to be publicly flogged. Ernesti refused to listen
to Krause's pleading, and even to Bach's;
refused to allow Krause to leave the school, and
when he absconded in order to evade what he
claimed to be not punishment but a public
disgrace, impounded his belongings and thirty

thalers held by the school to his credit.

Thus far Krause, in a complaint to the Council dated 26 July 1736. (The above-related events are not dated; but apparently took place in June.) On July 31 the Council ordered that Krause's thirty thalers should be restored to him. And there the matter might have rested, but for Ernesti; who insisted on appointing in Krause's place his namesake Johann Gottlieb Krause, who (it appears) was musically incompetent, and had some time previously been described by Bach, Ernesti not dissenting, as 'a dissolute hound'.

Now the Council's rules for the conduct of
the school declared 'it to be the Cantor's prerogative to select as Prefects those scholars whom
he regards as fit and competent', and this
prerogative had 'been exercised by successive
Cantors until now without interference on the
part of the Rectors.' So Bach stated his case
to the Council on Aug. 12; he had challenged
Ernesti on July 10 by sending to him the second
prefect (Kittler) with a message that he was to
take Krause's place because Bach found the
latter incompetent. Krause asked why he had

been displaced. He got his answer from Bach;
what exactly the latter told him is not known;
but he told Ernesti that Bach had degraded
him in order to show that the election of prefects
was entirely his affair. According to the strict
letter of the law Bach should have consulted
the Vorsteher of the school; but this he had not
done. The Vorsteher was inclined to support
Ernesti; and about the middle of July Bach
agreed to reinstate Krause. For some reason
he did not do so at once; then he was absent
from Leipzig until the end of the month; and

when he returned he still did nothing. So on Aug. 11 Ernesti wrote to him to say that unless he acted at once, he would himself reinstate Krause the next morning.

Early next day, Sunday August 12, Bach wrote to the Council the letter from which quotations have been given, asking them 'to instruct Rector Ernesti to act for the future in accordance with the usages and practice of the school.' He then visited Superintendent Deyling to discuss the matter. From Deyling he went on to the church, where he found the

service in progress with Krause, reinstated by
Ernesti, acting as first prefect. Bach turned him
out and put Kittler in his place; informed by
Ernesti (who had meanwhile consulted Deyling)
that the latter would not support his action, he
replied that 'he would not budge an inch from
his course, cost what it might.' Ernesti gave
orders that Krause and Kittler were to revert
to their positions as first and second prefect
respectively, and also forbade the choir to sing
under any substitute for Krause. Accordingly,
at Vespers in St. Nicholas' Bach found Krause

on duty again, and 'chased him from the
choir-gallery with much shouting and disturb-
ance.' This time, for fear of Ernesti, Kittler
would not take Krause's place; and when he
came to supper, Bach 'chased him from the
table.'

Next day (Aug. 13) Bach reported Sunday's
doings to the Council. Two days later he submitted a report on Krause's character and
musical efficiency — or rather, inefficiency;
since Bach declared that he 'could not beat
even the two ordinary measures $\left[\frac{4}{4} \text{ and } \frac{3}{4}\right]$

accurately.'

Two days later again (Aug. 17) Ernesti sent
in his reply: to judge from Terry's summary
(the full text is not at hand), that of a man
who knows himself to be in the wrong and is
reduced to picking holes. He made much of
Bach's failure to consult the Vorsteher about
the appointment of prefects, and stated (no
doubt truthfully) that this was Bach's habit.
He claimed that Krause had been satisfactory
as third and second prefect, and suggested
that the troubles of both the Krauses were in

reality due to the Cantor's absence from his
duty.

   The Council took no action; and on Sunday
Aug. 19 there was again disorder in the churches.
That day Bach wrote another letter to the Council,
to ask for a quick decision; but they took no
notice. Presumably some arrangement was
made to prevent further disturbances; but we
hear no more of the matter until on Sept. 13
Ernesti wrote to the Council alleging that it
was not impossible to bribe Bach ('an old
Species thaler made a discantist of one who

was no more a discantist than I am'), deny-
ing Krause's incompetence, and contradicting
Bach on other matters of fact. We are not in
a position to check the conflicting statements
of Cantor and Rector; but our judgement
goes against Ernesti if only because the man
who ventured to contradict Bach in matters
of elementary musical fact (not taste) must
have been a fool.

For five months we hear no more of this
affair, for reasons suggested below. In the
meantime (from the end of October) Bach's

peace of mind was further troubled by the mis-
doings of his son Bernhard, who had run up
debts at Mühlhausen and now removed thence
to Sangerhausen (see note 12, p. 89. Bach's letters
to Klemm, now in the Preussische Staatsbibliothek,
are printed in Zeitschrift der Sammelbände der
Internationalen Musik-Gesellschaft, Jhrg. III
(1902), pp. 351–60. Also Mühlhäuser Geschichts-
blätter, Jhrg. XXI (1920-1), pp. 78-9). Bernhard
passed his tests on 13 Jan. 1737, and was formally
appointed on April 4 to the Market Church (also
known as St. James').

PAGE 29

[26] Terry thinks that Bach's appointment at
Weissenfels dated from 1729, his honorary Capell-
meistership at Cöthen having ended with the
death of Prince Leopold. 'Herr Capell Meister
Bach' lodged at Weissenfels on 23 Feb. 1729, the
Duke's birthday.

The evidence is confusing and contradictory.
Walther (p.70) seems to have thought that Bach
became Capellmeister at Weissenfels soon after
he went to Leipzig.

When Bach's death was announced in St.

Thomas' (31 July 1750) the speaker described him
as 'Capellmeister to his Highness of Anhalt-
Cöthen'; and the author of the Genealogy says
he functioned as honorary Capellmeister to both
Weissenfels and Cöthen — this was about 1736.
Terry, however, states (p. 265, n. 2) that Bach
'received no appointment at Cöthen' from Leopold's successor.

The matter is of no great importance; but
it would be interesting to know exactly how and
when Bach was connected with Weissenfels, where
there was a good-sized organ with a pedalboard

extending to f', a note required for the Toccata
in F.

However all this may be Bach's appointment
at Weissenfels ended in 1736; the Duke died
on June 28, and his Capelle was disbanded.
This fact may have some connection with Bach's
obtaining, on Nov. 19, the long-coveted post of
Court Composer at Dresden. Perhaps Count
Kayserling had something to do with it; it was
he who paid 100 louis d'or for the Variations
named after his employee Goldberg, a harpsi-
chordist who had been a pupil of Bach's in 1733.

At all events, Kayserling received Bach's patent on Nov. 28, and on Dec. 1 Bach gave a recital at the Frauenkirche, Dresden, on a new organ by Silbermann. We do not know whether this recital had been arranged previously, or whether Bach took advantage of having been sent for by Kayserling to receive his patent (Bitter ii, 236; B.J. 1925). The recital referred to as having been given 'some time previously' was perhaps that of 1731 (p. 152).

We now return to the Krause controversy. His attempts to stir the Council to action having failed,

Bach decided to try the Consistorium (the ecclesiastical authority). In November 1736, on or
after the 10th, he prepared a letter to them; but
did not send it. Presumably the news of his
Court appointment led him to hope for Electoral
assistance. In this he was disappointed; and
on 12 Feb. 1737 he redated the November letter
(which is why the original date is uncertain) and
despatched it. Next day the Consistorium asked
the Council to attend to Bach's complaint without delay. But Krause was leaving the school
at Easter (Ap. 21); and the Council thought this

a heaven-sent opportunity of letting the matter
drop. They had, as a matter of fact, already
decided on Feb. 6 that Bach's claim to appoint
prefects was lawful; but they hesitated to condemn
Ernesti, and kept their decision secret until
April, when it was communicated to Ernesti
on the 6th, Bach on the 10th, and Superintendent
Deyling on the 20th. No further action was taken
until Aug. 21, when Bach wrote again to the
Consistorium. Still he failed to obtain satisfaction; so on Oct. 18 he appealed to the Elector,
who now at last took action. On Dec. 17 a

document was prepared demanding that Bach's
complaints should receive consideration. This
was before the Consistorium on 1 Feb. 1738 and the
Council on Feb. 5. We hear no more of the matter.
Some compromise must have been made; perhaps at the end of April, when the Elector had
occasion to visit Leipzig (27th), and heard, at
a University function, an adulatory cantata
with music by Bach — not by Görner. The old
controversy was revived, but settled in Bach's
favour by (one supposes) the University students,
who paid.

For the rest of his life Bach does not seem to have been seriously interfered with by his employers.

The school controversy was not Bach's only trouble during 1737. Johann Adolf Scheibe, son of Johann Scheibe who built the organs in St. Paul's and St. John's, Leipzig, had applied for the organistship of St. Thomas' in 1729. Görner was appointed; and Scheibe made no secret of his thinking that he had a grievance against Bach, who had been one of the judges. On 5 Mar. 1737 he started a periodical 'Der critische Musicus'

at Hamburg, in which (May 14) he made an
attack on Bach as a composer. J. A. Birnbaum
replied in a pamphlet published in Jan. 1738,
and the controversy dragged on into the following
year.

For the years 1738 to 1742 we have a few
intimate details of Bach's home life, thanks to
the letters of his cousin Johann Elias Bach
(Die Musik, 1912-13, pp. 3-19). Elias, thirty-three
years old in 1738, was a divinity student at
Leipzig University, and acted as tutor to the
three surviving sons of Bach's second marriage.

In the spring of 1738 Bernhard Bach absconded from Sangerhausen, where, as at Mühlhausen, he had got into debt. This affair is the subject of Bach's letters of May 24 and 26 to the Klemms. Bernhard, whose whereabouts were unknown to his father even as late as October, matriculated at Jena on 28 Jan. 1739, and died there of fever on May 27.

It is from Elias' letters of 10 Jan. and 28 Sept. 1739 that we learn of the publication of the Clavierübung, Part III, between those dates.

In July 1739 Friedemann visited his father
for a month's holiday, bringing with him two
celebrated lutanists. Bach's compositions for
the lute were probably inspired by this visit; and
a few months later he kept up the family tradition (p.3) by inventing the 'Lautenclavicymbel',
a combination of lute and harpsichord. A
specimen instrument was built for him by Zacharias Hildebrand.

About this time Prince Augustus Ludwig
of Cöthen visited Leipzig for a cure, and Bach
took part in a celebration of his birthday on

Aug. 3. He also produced a cantata for the
Elector's birthday on Oct. 7 (1739). He was
still conductor of the Collegium Musicum, an
orchestral society made up of University students,
with which he had been connected since 1729;
but he had practically ceased to compose for
the church, and was about to withdraw himself
almost completely from public music-making in
Leipzig. In the last ten years of his life he was
frequently out of Leipzig on various errands;
and at home he concentrated on organ and
clavier music, in particular on preparing some

few works for engraving and publication.

In 1741 Emanuel became accompanist to Frederick the Great, and Bach visited him in Berlin although Prussia was at war. He should have gone in June; but his visit was postponed until July, and was probably short. ened by an illness of Anna Magdalena's, of which he learnt from letters of Elias' dated Aug. 5 and 9. In November he and Elias visited Kayserling at Dresden. In 1742 the Goldberg Variations were published.

In 1744 Bach examined the organ at St.

Paul's, Leipzig, built by Johann Scheibe, the father of Johann Adolph Scheibe who had attacked Bach in 1737. The same year he completed the Second Part of the 'Forty-Eight' (defective autograph in the British Museum, Add. Ms. 35021). In 1746 (Aug. 7) he examined an organ at Zschortau (certificate in the British Museum, Add. MS. 33965, fol. 168); and on Sept. 27 he and Silbermann tested an organ by Zacharias Hildebrand at St. Wenceslas', Naumburg — the church to which Altnikol became organist, on Bach's recommendation, in 1748.

PAGE 30

[27] Emanuel had married in 1744; a son
was born to him on 30 Nov. 1745. This was the
first marriage in Bach's family; but it does
not appear that he visited Emanuel between
1741 and the spring of 1747. On this latter
occasion he took Friedemann with him. The
latter was probably the source for Forkel's account
of the visit to Frederick the Great; which is no
reason for regarding that account as strictly
trustworthy.

Most probably Frederick heard of Bach's
presence in Berlin from Emanuel. He seems to
have sent for Bach, who arrived in Potsdam
on the evening of Sunday May 7; the King
was just preparing for his usual evening concert. Bach was announced; the King exclaimed,
'Gentlemen, Old Bach is here,' abandoned with
his concert the more than military regularity of
his habits, and spent the evening listening
to Bach. The word 'pianoforte' is to be observed;
Frederick had a number of the early Silbermann
instruments.

On May 8 Bach gave an organ recital in the garrison church, Potsdam. According to one account it was this day that he extemporized the six-part fugue — the truth, as with the Marchand affair, is probably hopelessly buried beneath the inventions of Bach's sons. He returned to Berlin, and there inspected the new Opera House, astonishing his companions by deducing from the shape of the 'grand saloon' that it would give a whispering-gallery effect.

In June 1747 he joined Mizler's Society for the Promotion of Musical Science (p.214).

In 1748 Elias (since 29 May 1743 Cantor at Schweinfurt) asked Bach for a copy of 'the Prussian fuge' (some part of the Musical-ische Opfer, but which I cannot say at present). Bach replied on Oct. 6: 'justement to-day the edition is sold out. Only 100 copies were engraved, and most of them I gave away gratis to friends. However, between now and New Year's Fair more will be published, and if my cousin still desires an exemplar he should acquaint me with an opportunity to dispatch it, send me a thaler post, and it will be forwarded.'

Elias sent a cask of wine with his reply; and
on Nov. 2 Bach acknowledged the gift. Here is
his letter in full:

Worthy and respected cousin,

   Your letter, received yesterday, brings me
the good news that you and your dear wife are
well, and for the delectable cask of wine that
came with it accept my best thanks. Unfortunately the cask suffered a jar, or some other
accident, on the journey, for on examination
here it is found to be one-third empty and

contains, the Visitator declares, only six Kan-
nen. It is regrettable that the smallest drop
of so noble a gift of God should be wasted, but
I am none the less heartily obliged by my
worthy cousin's kind present. Pro nunc I am
not reellement in a position to reciprocate;
still, quod differtur non auffertur, and I hope
to find an opportunity to discharge my obligation.

   It is unfortunate that we live so far apart,
for else I should give myself the pleasure of
inviting her cousin to my daughter Lissgen's
wedding, which takes place in January 1749,

to the new Naumburg organist Herr Altnikol.
However, though for that reason, and because
of the inconvenient season, he cannot be present,
I will ask him to assist them with his good wishes,
and with the same I commend myself to my
good cousin's remembrance. With warmest
greetings to you from all here, I remain

      Your Honour's devoted and faithful cousin +
        servant to command,

          Joh. Seb. Bach.

Leipzig, 2 November 1748.

  P.S. Magister Birnbaum was buried six

weeks ago.

P. M. Though my good cousin offers to send
me more of the same liqueur, I must decline
on account of the heavy charges at this end.
The carriage was 16 gr., delivery 2 gr., Visitator
2 gr., provincial excise 5 gr. 3 pfg., general
excise 3 gr. So my cousin may calculate that
the wine cost me nearly 5 gr. a measure, a too
expensive present!

A Monsieur J. E. Bach, Chanteur [Cantor]
et Inspecteur des Gymnasiastes de la Ville
Imperialle à Schweinfourth, Franqué Coburg.

Lissgen (Elisabeth Juliana Friederica Bach) married Johann Christoph Altnikol, who had been a pupil of Bach's (see also p. 187), on 20 Jan. 1749.

In the early summer of 1749 Bach was evidently ill; Terry thinks, apparently on the evidence of Taylor the 'eye-doctor', that he had a stroke about May. In June one Harrer was tested with a view to his being appointed in Bach's place; but the latter recovered.

On 12 May 1749 one Biedermann, Rector of the Freiberg Gymnasium, saw fit to denounce

the study of music on the grounds that it was
bad for the morals : he chose Caligula and Nero
as examples. A controversy broke out ; one Schröter,
a member of Mizler's Society, wrote a reply,
apparently at Bach's request ; this was approved
by Bach and published in 1750 (Bitter iii, 236).
Schröter then found that his text had been altered, and accused Bach. The latter wrote on
May 26 to an intermediary to say that he could
not at present write to Schröter, but was not
to blame for the alterations.

PAGE 32

[28] The above-mentioned letter to Schröter was probably dictated, not written by Bach himself; though this is not known for certain. It is unlikely, however, that by May 1750 Bach's sight would have allowed him to write.

The 'eye-doctor' whom he consulted, perhaps ? at the end of 1749, was the Chevalier John Taylor, an English charlatan. According to Terry, Taylor was again in Leipzig in Jan. 1750, on his way from Vienna to Mecklenburg. Ilse Hecht (Musical Times, March 1938, p.175) shows that he

see M & L April 1938

was lecturing in Leipzig on Mar. 28. It happens
that Bach's ability to write at this time has some
bearing on the text of the 'Vom Himmel hoch' Variations; and it is unfortunate that we cannot
date his operations.

It has been held that the autograph text of
the Variations dates from 1750, and is therefore later than that of the engraved edition,
which apparently was published about 1747.
I believe that this theory — and with it the idea
that the Autograph text is superior — is con-
clusively disproved by a correction in the last

bars of the Canon by Augmentation ; but it
would be useful to know for certain that Bach
was incapable of writing after Jan. 1750.

Whether the following famous story has some
early authority, or is simply a (legitimate)
deduction from the state of the MS., I do not
know.

In his last days Bach dictated to Altnikol
an expanded and drastically revised version
of the Orgelbüchlein prelude 'Wenn wir in
höchsten Nöthen sein' (When we are in deepest
need). But Bach was not now thinking of that

hymn; he had in his mind one even more
appropriate to his condition:

> Before Thy throne, my God, I stand,
> Myself, my all, are in Thy hand;
>
> . . . .
>
> Grant that my end may worthy be,
> And that I wake Thy face to see,
> Thyself for evermore to know!
> Amen, Amen, God grant it so!
>
> (tr. C.S. Terry)

and he had the prelude headed accordingly,
'Vor deinen Thron tret ich hiemit'. It is very

generally overrated, on account of its sentimental
interest. For some reason only part of it appears
in the MS.; the complete work was published
with the Art of Fugue, apparently to compensate
for the incompleteness of that work.

Bach was buried on 31 July 1750 near the
south wall of St. John's Church. On the 29th
the Council had already met to consider the
appointment of Harrer in his place; they had
the grace to defer their decision until Aug. 7.
On this 29th they had referred to Bach as 'the
Cantor of St. Thomas' School, or rather Capell-

Director Bach'; and one of them said, 'The School needs a Cantor not a Capellmeister; although certainly he ought to understand music.' These words were uttered by one Stieglitz. It is well that the name of this typical Councillor should be remembered.

The exact site of Bach's grave was soon forgotten; but in 1894 opportunity occurred to make excavations, and on Oct. 22 there was unearthed what has been accepted as Bach's skeleton. The remains were placed beneath the altar of the church.

PAGE 35

[29] The Clavierübung, Part I, consists of the six Partitas; these were published singly, one each year from 1726 onwards (p. 138), and then all together in 1731. According to Forkel, they were in some demand.

The original edition of the Nekrolog has 'pages' (Seiten) for 'suites' (Suiten).

Part II, the Italian Concerto and Overture in B minor (Overture here means Suite: the work is that which includes the 'Echo' movement), appeared in 1735; Part III (the Catechism Preludes) in 1739; and the 'Aria with Thirty Variations', Part IV , in 1742.

The Six Preludes, known as the 'Schüblers' from the publisher's name, probably appeared in 1746. Five of them are arrangements of vocal movements from the Cantatas, and the sixth is presumably a similar arrangement from a lost Cantata.

The Canonic Variations probably appeared about 1747. The dedicatory letter of the Musical Offering is dated 7 July 1747 (I think only part of the work was engraved at this date). The

Art of Fugue, partly engraved before Bach's death, was published, I think, in 1751; there was a second edition.

PAGE 38

30 The following identifications and remarks may be useful:

2 'Masses' — includes the short Lutheran Masses as well as the B minor. 'Oratorios' — only the Christmas Oratorio is well known under that title; but Cantata 11 is also known as the Ascension Oratorio, and I believe there is an Easter one. The Magnificat referred to

is that in D, not Cantata 10.

3   Five Passions. Emanuel may have included the St. Luke Passion, now rejected as spurious. Only two genuine Passions are now known.

4   Not all the Motets are for double choir.

6   These are the Sonatas.

8   Probably the Orgelbüchlein.

9   The Forty-Eight: Part I 1722, Part II 1744.

11   The 'English' Suites.

12   The 'French' Suites.

13   'without bass'; i.e., without figured bass,

unaccompanied.

In an undated letter to Forkel (Bach-Urkunden) Emanuel adds to this list the Inventions and Six Short Preludes (all for clavier). His catalogue seems to consist chiefly of works in his own possession. We have a fair idea of the MSS. that came into his hands, from a list of (MS.) music that his widow published — the MSS. were for sale. The British Museum has a copy of this list.

PAGE 39

3¹ Maria Barbara Bach was born 20 Oct.

1684, married Sebastian at Dornheim 17 Oct. 1707, and was buried 4 July 1720.

[32] Wilhelm Friedemann Bach was born 22 Nov. 1710; began his musical education 22 Jan. 1720, with the Clavierbüchlein; became organist of St. Sophia's, Dresden, in 1733 (p. 155); moved to Halle in 1746; later resigned that post, took to drink, and finally died in poverty 1 July 1784.

Carl Philipp Emanuel Bach was born 8 Mar. 1714; became a student at Frankfurt

1734; accompanist to Frederick the Great
1741; Capellmeister at Hamburg, 1767; died
15 Dec. 1788.

PAGE 40

33 Anna Magdalena Wilcken (the name is
spelt in several different ways) was baptized
22 Sept. 1701. She was a singer ('a very clear
soprano' says Bach in his letter to Erdmann)
and was employed as such at the court of
Anhalt-Zerbst, and then from the autumn of
1720 at Cöthen. She had been to Cöthen as a
visitor before that time. She retained her pos-

ition as a soprano after her marriage, which took place on 3 Dec. 1721. Bach made two music-books for her, the Clavierbüchlein in 1722 and the Notenbuch in 1725.

PAGE 41

34 Gottfried Heinrich (d. 1763) was half-witted. Elisabeth's marriage has been referred to (pp. 193, 196); Altnikol died in 1759. Johann Christoph, born 21 June 1732, took up his position as Chamber Musician early in 1750, and became known as the Bückeburg Bach. He died 26 Jan. 1795. Johann Christian, born 5 Sept. 1735, studied in

Italy, became an opera composer, and died in London 1 Jan. 1782. Johanna Carolina died in 1781; Regina Susanna survived until 1809.

Anna Magdalena's own children were in 1750 too young to be able to support her; and her step-children, to their lasting disgrace, took no pains to do so. She lived on as an alms-woman, and on 27 Feb. 1760 received a pauper's funeral.

PAGE 48

35 The organ referred to was that in St. John's, Leipzig; for the 'certain circumstances' see

pp. 186, 181.

PAGE 49

36 'schönen und nie gehörten Erfindungen im Orgelspielen'. I do not understand this.

37 Bach was also a string-player. In private music-makings he played the viola, because it placed him in the middle of the harmony. His compositions show that he had a thorough knowledge of string technique.

He is also said to have practised music-engraving; and certainly parts of the Clavier-

übung, Part III, are engraved in a 'hand' very
similar to Bach's.

PAGE 50

[38] Here begins Mizler's contribution to the
Nekrolog.

Lorentz Christoph Mizler graduated at
Leipzig in 1734. In 1736 he started the 'Neu
eröffnete musicalische Bibliothek', and in
1738 founded his Society. The members were
men who held some sort of musical position
and were not merely executants. They did not
meet, but circulated music and articles among

themselves and contributed theoretical papers to the Musicalischer Bibliothek. The Society had a library, on whose walls were hung portraits of the members; these they had to present when they were elected.

Bach's portrait was the work of the Dresden Court painter E. G. Haussmann. When the Society broke up, the portrait went to the Thomasschule; it is now in the old Rathaus. It shows Bach holding in his hand the canon referred to in the text. This is the most familiar portrait; but one suspects that it is far less characteristic than that which was discovered by Fritz Volbach in 1904 (Die Musik, Jahrg. IX, Oct.-Dec. 1909, p. 107.; reproductions in Schweitzer and Parry).

Emanuel's opinion of the Society's 'deep theoretical speculations' is made indecently clear by his remarks quoted on p. xiv.

It is supposed that Bach's diploma piece was the Canonic Variations. Unfortunately, the date of publication of the engraved text cannot be closely determined, which makes matters no easier for the editor, whose first business is to find out whether the engraved or the autograph text is the later. My own view is that when Bach had made his usual rough draft of the work, he fair-copied it twice: one copy (lost) was for circulation in the Society, and was itself copied: the other, for his own use, he made in the MS. that already contained the Organ Sonatas and some of (what we call) the Eighteen Chorale-Preludes. Later he decided to engrave the work, and revised it for that purpose.

Mizler's words (p.51) are important. It will be seen that he distinguishes between the 'completely worked out' version presented to the Society

and that which was engraved 'afterwards'.
The meaning of the words 'completely worked
out' is clear enough: the copy supplied to the
Society was written out in full, whereas in the
engraved edition the answering parts of the
canons are omitted (perhaps to save expense).
The missing parts, being exact transpositions
(almost)
of the leaders, could easily be supplied by anyone who wished to make himself a copy to play
from.

PAGE 51

39 Cf. Bitter iii, 211. It is a triple Canon in six

parts — whatever that may mean. In the portrait and the Nekrolog it appears in puzzle-canon form; a full working-out is in C.L. Hilgenfeldt, Johann Sebastian Bachs Leben, Wirken und Werke, Leipzig 1850, Table 3.

The text given here (p. [63]) is copied from Terry. I have not had access either to the original edition of the Nekrolog or even to the B.G.

PAGE [67]

4° Johann Gottfried Walther (1684 – 1748) was organist of the Town Church at Weimar from 1707 until his death. He was a composer

of some ability, his speciality being organ
chorale-preludes; and his Musical Dictionary
is an important work of reference.

Walther and Bach were distantly and ob-
scurely related through the Lämmerhirt family,
and were intimate, it seems, while Bach was
in Weimar. Bach stood godfather to Walther's
eldest son on 26 Sept. 1712. Forkel has an
anecdote of their friendly rivalry at the clavier.

From the brevity and tone of Walther's article
Spitta deduced that he and Bach must have
become estranged; but the evidence seems in-

sufficient, and in any case the matter is of no particular importance.

PAGE 69

4¹ The date is correct.

4² The word 'came' and on p. 70 'here' show how an author may give away information about himself quite unconsciously. Cf. preface to the Saga of the Ere-dwellers, Saga Library II.

PAGE 70

43 See p. 174.

PAGE 71

44 See p. 204.

45 Perhaps Walther got this idea from Bach
himself. See p. 81.

46 H is, of course, b natural; and b is b flat.
The ticks indicate pitch — b' is middle b flat
on the piano keyboard.

The clavier Prelude and Fugue on BACH
is of doubtful authenticity; Bach seems to have
used his own name only once: as the third
subject of the unfinished Contrapunctus in
the Art of Fugue.

PAGE [73]

47 The translation is taken from the facsimile

in Bach-Urkunden; that is to say, from the
copy of the Genealogy that belonged to Emanuel and was partly brought up to date by him
before he handed it over to Forkel.

The great puzzle about the Genealogy is that
on the one hand the phrase "according to God's
holy Will" leaves us in little doubt that the
wording is Sebastian's; but if this is so, we
have to account for his giving a wrong date for
his own first organ appointment, and not
knowing where or when his eldest brother was
born, or when he died.

The Genealogy contains 53 entries dealing with male Bachs from Veit to Sebastian's children. It must have been compiled about 1736, since it records the birth of Johann Christian (5 Sept. 1735), but not Sebastian's appointment as Court Composer (19 Nov. 1736).

The passage in { } is an insertion by Emmanuel, made presumably in 1774 or 5, when he handed the MS. over to Forkel. It will be observed that he gives a wrong date for Bach's death.

PAGE 75

48 So the MS. Read 1703. Cf. p. 94.

49 See p. 101.

PAGE 76

50 See p. 174.

51 Read 28 July.

POSTSCRIPT

ANYONE who has read the Dedicatory Note and Introduction will see that this book has been meant to be divers things at sundry times; and now is perhaps something quite different again. The fact is, it has been put together in bits and pieces. The preliminary matter was written after the translation, but long before the notes were finished; and fair-copying and annotation went on together. Hence certain inconsistencies.

Now that the job is done I can describe
the scope of the Notes more accurately. They
are a summary of Terry's Biography — i.e.
of the latest modern research. A few incidents,
unlikely to be of importance to me and of no
special interest to anyone, I have left altogether unmentioned. I am afraid I have
included an exasperating number of mere
dates; but they are the editor's bread and
butter, and I only wish we had more of them.

Glancing over the whole to remove the grosser

errors, I have found one or two points that
need comment. There are probably others.

On p. xvii read Musicalisches (for Musik-).

On p. 12, line 7, 'indirectly' would be better
than 'incidentally'.

Page 15, line 1: 'In 1703 he came to Weimar.'
See note 42, p. 221. On this principle Emanuel or Agricola (or both) wrote this passage
at Weimar. But I doubt it. Probably they
regarded Bach's move to Weimar as a return
(to Thuringia from far-off Lüneburg), and
for that reason used the word 'came'. A

warning, perhaps, to textual critics; like Knox's
Essays in Satire; though of course I might
find, if I were in a position to make the
necessary investigations, that Agricola held
a post at Weimar at some time or other.
Emanuel certainly did not.

Page 32: 'a quarter to nine'; so Terry.
I suppose he knew what 'nach einem Viertel
auf 9 Uhr' means; I don't.

Pages 34 and 37. I suppose there is some
significance in the use of 'vor' instead of
'über'; but I don't know what it is.

POSTSCRIPT   231

Page 181. For Adolf read Adolph.
(That Man again!)

BEGUN AT BEDFORD in October 1941;
continued at Market Warsop, and finished
19 Jan. 1942.

                    Walter Emery

Music and Books published by Travis & Emery Music Bookshop:

Anon.: Hymnarium Sarisburense, cum Rubris et Notis Musicus
Agricola, Johann Friedrich from Tosi: Anleitung zur Singkunst. (Faksimile 1757)
Bach, C.P.E.: edited W. Emery: Nekrolog or Obituary Notice of J.S. Bach.
Bateson, Naomi Judith: Alcock of Salisbury
Bathe, William: A Briefe Introduction to the Skill of Song
Bax, Arnold: Symphony #5, Arranged for Piano Four Hands by Walter Emery
Burney, Charles: The Present State of Music in France and Italy
Burney, Charles: The Present State of Music in Germany, The Netherlands ...
Burney, Charles: An Account of the Musical Performances ... Handel
Burney, Karl: Nachricht von Georg Friedrich Handel's Lebensumstanden.
Cobbett, W.W.: Cobbett's Cyclopedic Survey of Chamber Music. (2 vols.)
Corrette, Michel: Le Maitre de Clavecin
Crimp, Bryan: Dear Mr. Rosenthal ... Dear Mr. Gaisberg ...
Crimp, Bryan: Solo: The Biography of Solomon
d'Indy, Vincent: Beethoven: Biographie Critique
d'Indy, Vincent: Beethoven: A Critical Biography
d'Indy, Vincent: César Franck (in French)
Frescobaldi, Girolamo: D'Arie Musicali per Cantarsi. Primo Libro & Secondo Libro.
Geminiani, Francesco: The Art of Playing the Violin.
Handel; Purcell; Boyce; Geene et al: Calliope or English Harmony: Volume First.
Hawkins, John: A General History of the Science and Practice of Music (5 vols.)
Herbert-Caesari, Edgar: The Science and Sensations of Vocal Tone
Herbert-Caesari, Edgar: Vocal Truth
Hopkins and Rimboult: The Organ. Its History and Construction.
Hunt, John: Adam to Webern: the recordings of von Karajan
Isaacs, Lewis: Hänsel and Gretel. A Guide to Humperdinck's Opera.
Isaacs, Lewis: Königskinder (Royal Children) A Guide to Humperdinck's Opera.
Lacassagne, M. l'Abbé Joseph : Traité Général des élémens du Chant.
Lascelles (née Catley), Anne: The Life of Miss Anne Catley.
Mainwaring, John: Memoirs of the Life of the Late George Frederic Handel
Malcolm, Alexander: A Treaty of Music: Speculative, Practical and Historical
Marx, Adolph Bernhard: Die Kunst des Gesanges, Theoretisch-Practisch
May, Florence: The Life of Brahms
Mellers, Wilfrid: Angels of the Night: Popular Female Singers of Our Time
Mellers, Wilfrid: Bach and the Dance of God
Mellers, Wilfrid: Beethoven and the Voice of God
Mellers, Wilfrid: Caliban Reborn - Renewal in Twentieth Century Music
Mellers, Wilfrid: François Couperin and the French Classical Tradition

Travis & Emery Music Bookshop
17 Cecil Court, London, WC2N 4EZ, United Kingdom.
Tel. (+44) 20 7240 2129

Music and Books published by Travis & Emery Music Bookshop:

Mellers, Wilfrid: Harmonious Meeting
Mellers, Wilfrid: Le Jardin Retrouvé, The Music of Frederic Mompou
Mellers, Wilfrid: Music and Society, England and the European Tradition
Mellers, Wilfrid: Music in a New Found Land: ... ... American Music
Mellers, Wilfrid: Romanticism and the Twentieth Century (from 1800)
Mellers, Wilfrid: The Masks of Orpheus: ... ... the Story of European Music.
Mellers, Wilfrid: The Sonata Principle (from c. 1750)
Mellers, Wilfrid: Vaughan Williams and the Vision of Albion
Panchianio, Cattuffio: Rutzvanscad Il Giovine
Pearce, Charles: Sims Reeves, Fifty Years of Music in England.
Pettitt, Stephen: Philharmonia Orchestra: complete discography
Playford, John: An Introduction to the Skill of Musick.
Purcell, Henry et al: Harmonia Sacra ... The First Book, (1726)
Purcell, Henry et al: Harmonia Sacra ... Book II (1726)
Quantz, Johann: Versuch einer Anweisung die Flöte traversiere zu spielen.
Rameau, Jean-Philippe: Code de Musique Pratique, ou Methodes.
Rastall, Richard: The Notation of Western Music.
Rimbault, Edward: The Pianoforte, Its Origins, Progress, and Construction.
Rousseau, Jean Jacques: Dictionnaire de Musique
Rubinstein, Anton : Guide to the proper use of the Pianoforte Pedals.
Sainsbury, John S.: Dictionary of Musicians. Vol. 1. (1825). 2 vols.
Simpson, Christopher: A Compendium of Practical Musick in Five Parts
Spohr, Louis: Autobiography
Spohr, Louis: Grand Violin School
Tans'ur, William: A New Musical Grammar; or The Harmonical Spectator
Terry, Charles Sanford: Four-Part Chorals of J.S. Bach. (German & English)
Terry, Charles Sanford: Joh. Seb. Bach, Cantata Texts, Sacred and Secular.
Terry, Charles Sanford: The Origins of the Family of Bach Musicians.
Tosi, Pierfrancesco: Opinioni de' Cantori Antichi, e Moderni
Van der Straeten, Edmund: History of the Violoncello, The Viol da Gamba ...
Van der Straeten, Edmund: History of the Violin, Its Ancestors... (2 vols.)
Walther, J. G.: Musicalisches Lexikon ober Musicalische Bibliothec (1732)

Travis & Emery Music Bookshop
17 Cecil Court, London, WC2N 4EZ, United Kingdom.
Tel. (+44) 20 7240 2129

www.ingramcontent.com/pod-product-compliance
Lightning Source LLC
Chambersburg PA
CBHW020456100426
42812CB00024B/2676